Jesus and Creativity

Works by Gordon D. Kaufman

Relativism, Knowledge and Faith (1960)

The Context of Decision (1961)

Systematic Theology: A Historicist Perspective (1968)

God the Problem (1972)

An Essay on Theological Method
(1975; third edition, 1995)

Nonresistance and Responsibility,
and Other Mennonite Essays (1979)

The Theological Imagination:
Constructing the Concept of God (1981)

Theology for a Nuclear Age (1985)

In Face of Mystery: A Constructive Theology (1993)

God—Mystery—Diversity:
Christian Theology in a Pluralistic World (1996)

In the beginning . . . Creativity (2004)

Jesus
and Creativity

Gordon D. Kaufman

Fortress Press
Minneapolis

JESUS AND CREATIVITY

The author would like to greatfully acknowledge Harvard University Press, who gave permission draw on *In Face of Mystery: A Constructive Theology* (1993), especially in ch. 3 of this book.

Cover image: *Vines*, by Lou Wall © Lou Wall/Corbis.
Cover design: Kevin van der Leek Design, Inc., and James Korsmo
Book design: James Korsmo

Library of Congress Cataloging-in-Publication Data

Kaufman, Gordon D.
  Jesus and creativity / Gordon D. Kaufman.
    p. cm.
  Includes bibliographical references and index.
  ISBN-13: 978-0-8006-3798-9 (alk. paper)
  ISBN-10: 0-8006-3798-4 (alk. paper)
  1. Jesus Christ—Person and offices. 2. Creation. 3. Philosophical theology. I. Title.
  BT203.K38 2006
  232—dc22
                                    2006016826

10   09   08   07   06   1   2   3   4   5   6   7   8   9   10

For
Adele *and* Jennifer
Thanks!

Contents

When Jesus was crucified, his followers saw that he could never carry to fulfillment the mission of the Jewish people as they conceived it. . . . He was not the messiah they had expected, and, so far as they could see, he was no messiah at all. The depth of devotion and the glory of the vision they had possessed made their disillusionment all the more bitter and devastating. . . . They reached that depth of despair which comes when all that seems to give hope to human existence is seen to be an illusion. . . .

After about the third day, however, when the numbness of the shock had worn away, something happened. The life-transforming creativity previously known only in fellowship with Jesus began again to work in the fellowship of the disciples. It was risen from the dead. . . . What rose from the dead was not the man Jesus; it was creative power. It was the living God that works in time.

Henry Nelson Wieman (1946)

preface

In the Fourth Gospel we read: "God so loved the world that he gave his only Son, so that everyone who believes in him may not perish but may have eternal life" (John 3:16). This much-loved sentence sums up beautifully a central theme of traditional Christian faith. But for many thoughtful Christians today, sentences like this—very common in Christian speech and writing—scarcely make sense. Though they may be lovely poetry, whether they tell us anything about the real world with which we must come to terms every day may seem dubious. The metaphors get so thick and heavy in this sentence that it is hard to know just what they convey. Consider some of the problems:

What does it mean to say that God "loves" the world? If one considers nature "red in tooth and claw"—as often viewed these days on television nature programs—one can hardly help wondering what kind of love this could be. We know something about human love, and we cherish that; but what can it mean to say that the creator of this vast complex universe, fourteen billion years old, *loves* it? Can we really apply the word "love" to such a mysterious, unknowable reality as the creator of the universe? And what can it mean to say that this creator has a "Son"? We know what it means for humans to have children and to love their children—but how can we meaningfully apply such *creaturely* words as "love" and "son" to the origin of all that is? Doesn't this kind of language suggest that God is basically like some unimaginably huge and powerful human being? Does that make sense?

And one wonders whether it makes sense, any more, to declare that humans will not perish at the end of their lives. All living creatures—as we think of them today—come into being and in due course pass away. How can such an impossible exception to this fundamental characteristic of all life, as we know it, even be imagined? Where could all these billions of people be? And what could the phrase "*eternal* life" possibly be referring to?

If one stops to think about it, this sort of traditional Christian talk seems quite strange today, indeed very problematic. It is true, of course, that many Christians say they believe all these things and more. And it is also true that these ways of thinking and speaking have been very important historically, and without them we would never have heard of Jesus at all. But Christian theology has always warned of the dangers of religious language. And today many find it difficult to make sense out of much of this kind of Christian speech. This book about Jesus and Christian faith is written for people who are puzzled about these sorts of things. Instead of the traditional ways of understanding Christian faith, it proposes a different option for thinking about Jesus and his significance. The world in which these early metaphors and ideas were developed was quite different from our own, and what seemed to make good sense in that world often is virtually unintelligible in ours. The language and metaphors that we find in John 3:16 were quite intelligible in the world in which John was writing; it was powerful language, and for many generations it expressed and explained clearly the heart of Christian faith. But in the last several centuries, as our cultural and intellectual worlds have changed drastically, many modern persons—including many Christians—have found it quite difficult to understand this kind of speech. How should we understand and express that faith today?

I do not attempt in this book to explain the words of John 3:16 or other similar difficult-to-understand texts. Instead, we shall—starting from the ground up, so to speak—attempt to think through and make intelligible for our modern/postmodern time and world the story of Jesus. At many points we will be using quite different language and metaphors and ways of thinking than we find in the traditional texts; and the image/story of Jesus that unfolds before us will be quite different in significant ways from the traditional picture. But it will be one, I think, that many today will find freeing and illuminating, an appropriate way to understand the legacy of this figure who is at the very center of Christian faith.

Before we can take that up, I need to make a few remarks about God. Instead of continuing to imagine God as The Creator, a kind of personlike reality who has brought everything into being, I have for some years been developing and elaborating a conception of God as simply the *creativity* that has brought forth the world and all its contents, from the Big Bang all the way down to the present. Imagining God as creativity enables Christian thinkers to be much more attuned to what the modern sciences have been teaching us about our lives and the world in which we live. It makes it possible to bridge the divide often felt between religious faith and our scientific knowledges. This idea of creativity—originally worked out in my book entitled *In Face of Mystery: A Constructive Theology* (Kaufman 1993)—was developed further in a recently published book, *In the beginning . . . Creativity* (Kaufman 2004). Since then I have come to realize that this second book is really part 1 of what is in fact a two-part set on *God as Creativity*. And I have written this companion book entitled *Jesus and Creativity* (also free-standing like part 1) as part 2 of that series. In this book a new interpretation of Jesus for today is worked out. I thought this was what I was presenting when I wrote the chapters on Jesus and the trinity in *In Face of Mystery*. However, in this new book I found it necessary to develop a quite different interpretation of the significance of Jesus, one that makes some important changes from my earlier christological and trinitarian reflections.

This book has four chapters. The conception of God as *creativity* (instead of The Creator) requires us to rethink completely the traditional way of understanding Jesus. Chapter 1, entitled "Reconceiving the Jesus-Trajectory," presents an introductory discussion of this matter. In early accounts of the Jesus-story we can detect suggestions of a kind of movement or development in the way Jesus' followers understood who he was. This movement begins with the period of Jesus' ministry on earth and his crucifixion; that picture, however, became drastically changed by their belief in his resurrection; and this development finally culminated, then, in Jesus' elevation to deity. That these things did not occur until after Jesus' death is clearly implied in Romans 1:4, where Paul states that Jesus "was declared to be Son of God with power . . . by resurrection from the dead." Paul is telling us that an important development in the Jesus-story—that he is "Son of God with power"—did not occur until *after* his death, in connection with his followers' understanding of what they called his resurrection. As we shall see in chapters 1 and 2, given this new understanding, it is not surprising that Christian thinking about Jesus moved on into quasi-divine—even fully divine!—terms sometime after his death. I call these developments Jesus-trajectory$_1$. From today's historical, cultural, and intellectual perspectives, this picture raises many serious problems. In chapter 1, I examine this development of Jesus-trajectory$_1$ and some of the problems it raises, and then offer a significantly different account—Jesus-trajectory$_2$, I call it—that should prove more comprehensible to many women and men today. The rest of the book then elaborates and unpacks an interpretation based on Jesus-trajectory$_2$.

As we shall see, in Jesus-trajectory$_1$ we are presented with a story of Jesus that presupposes a dualistic understanding of the world. We humans live down here on earth—with some very real joys and achievements, but also many problems and difficulties and failures; there is, however, another world above called *heaven*, where God's reign is perfect and complete. In the biblical story it is from heaven that God's son Jesus came to earth, and it is heaven to which he ascended again in triumph after his death and resurrection. Many today would no longer regard this dualistic world-picture as true literally, but this raises the question, then, of how the Jesus-story is to be understood. Every contemporary interpretation of Jesus deals with this problem in one way or another, often without explaining how these matters are being addressed. New Testament scholar Rudolf Bultmann was famous for having set out explicitly his program of "demythologizing" the gospel story. Bultmann, however, retains the basic dualism of the old mythic world-picture when he declares that the "other side"—some other reality outside this life, this world of our experience—is more important than anything on "this side," since it is the real foundation of life and its meaning (see Kaufman 1993:325f.; Bultmann 1958). In my opinion, to retain the deep dualism of the biblical version of the Jesus-story is to remain at odds with our contemporary understanding of the world and human life in the world; and therefore—in Jesus-trajectory$_2$—I set out a version of the Jesus-story in which all the significant events are understood to have taken place here on planet Earth.

I need to make it clear right away that this book is not one more attempt to recover the historical Jesus and the beginnings of Christianity. I am not a New Testament scholar, nor am I a historian of ancient Christianity. Though I have done some reading in these fields over the years, I am in no position to make a well-argued historical analysis of the beginnings of the Christian movement and must defer to other writers on these matters; nor am I in a position to judge which of the several current portraits of Jesus are most historically credible. So I have attempted to avoid these highly contested technical issues as much as possible and have presented what I take to be plausible readings of the historical materials and the biblical texts that I discuss. I am a theologian trying to develop in this book an interpretation of Jesus that will be meaningful to Christians and others who today find some of the traditional claims about Jesus—such as those just mentioned about his deity—simply unbelievable, perhaps unintelligible. I hold that if we think of God as *creativity* (rather than as The Creator)—and in connection with this change give up the basic dualism of the Jesus-story as we have received it—we will be in a position to develop a plausible and meaningful interpretation of the significance of Jesus for today.

For many years I have maintained that if we examine carefully some of the concepts and metaphors that are often taken for granted in theological thinking (concepts such as "The Creator"), we may be able to develop new related concepts (such as "creativity") that will enable us to think in strikingly different ways about important matters. In this book we will be working largely on *conceptual* matters of this sort—trying to develop metaphors and concepts that will enable Christians today (and others interested) to think more plausibly and fittingly about the significance of Jesus. Though it is necessary, of course, to consider biblical materials here and to take into account some historical data, my objective is not basically to present new arguments on historical matters but rather to develop concepts that will enable us to think freshly about the story and significance of Jesus. To accomplish this it will be necessary to

introduce some metaphors and concepts different from those traditionally employed, as well as to understand differently the pattern of events
in the Jesus-story.

The concept of *creativity*—elaborated in some detail in *In the beginning . . . Creativity*—will be crucial in our work here. We do not know
why or how creativity comes about: it is a profound *mystery*. The mark
that identifies the occurrence of creativity is its *consequence*: something
strikingly *new*, something *transformative* has come into being and has
become a significant feature of the ongoing world. There is much
creativity manifest in Jesus' ministry; and his crucifixion and what was
called his resurrection also proved to be exceedingly creative events: they
led to the missionary activities of the disciples and others, who carried
the inspiring Jesus-story around the Roman Empire and beyond. And
those activities in turn created a movement that eventually became
worldwide, with creative social and cultural consequences of many
different sorts throughout subsequent history. It is this enormously
creative historical movement, beginning with Jesus and the Jesus-story,
that I call Jesus-trajectory$_2$. This book presents a theological reading of
this distinctly different Jesus-trajectory.

Chapter 2, entitled "Christology: Jesus as Norm," follows with an
analysis central for the constructive argument of this book. (Christology
is reflection on the person and significance of Jesus.) I take for granted
here the understanding of God as that *creativity* that is manifest throughout our developing evolutionary cosmos and especially manifest as we
consider the evolutionary emergence of *life* on planet Earth and the
eventual emergence of human *history* and *historicity*. This thinking opens
up new ways to understand Jesus' significance, on the one hand, and
Jesus' special relation to God (to *creativity*) on the other. These are understandings that do not invoke either a two-worlds cosmic framework or
the traditional two-natures conception of Jesus. In chapter 3 the notion
of "humans as biohistorical beings"—an understanding with which we
will be working throughout—is sketched. This conception enables us
to bring scientific knowledge of the biological base of our humanness
into intimate interconnection with our profound human concerns about
social, cultural, and religious values and meanings, practices, and institutions; it thus provides us with a way to bring our basic theological concerns with Jesus and God into significant interconnection with central

features of today's understanding of our humanness. Finally, in chapter 4 the overall theological conclusions about the significant connections of Jesus with creativity (God) are summed up, and the claim is made that this christology can inspire us to address in fresh ways some of the most serious new problems that humans must today face—particularly the ecological crisis and the challenging problem of melding ourselves into one integrated human world despite the enormous pluralism and divisiveness of our long and painful histories.

This book presents an understanding of Jesus' relationship to God quite different from the traditional one in which Jesus is presented as Son of God, as second person of the trinity, and so on. The concept of God employed here—God as *creativity*—is different from, though importantly related to, that found in traditional Christian faith and thinking. It both enables and requires us to ask questions about Jesus' creativity and what that creativity can mean for our understanding of him and his relation to God. It is my hope that the theological proposals made in this book will enable many Christians—as well as other interested persons—to see the Christian symbol of Jesus in a new light, a light that opens up and strengthens their faith as they seek to come to terms *creatively* with the enormous problems we humans must today address.

One could say that it took much of my life as a theologian to write this book. In 1976, having completed my *Essay on Theological Method*, I decided to begin employing the idea of theology as "imaginative construction" (see Kaufman 1995) by writing a new book on christology. But when I began to think about that book, I ran into a difficult problem. As we have noted, in Christian traditions Jesus Christ is usually understood as at once both divine and human, the "God-man." I had some ideas about what it is to be human; but what could it possibly mean to think of a human as *divine?* One would have to know what God is in order to deal with that question, and that was a big problem for me at that time (I had recently published a book entitled *God the Problem* [Kaufman 1972]). It became obvious to me that I would be in no position to work on christology until I became much clearer on how I understood God. As it turned out, it took me about eighteen years to work through that problem: *In Face of Mystery* (1993)—with its presentation of God as simply *creativity* (rather than The Creator)—was the result. That book includes chapters sketching views on christology and the trinity, chapters which at that time I believed to be consistent with thinking of God as creativity. But the story turned out to be not quite over. About ten years later, after I had spelled out the idea of God-as-creativity in a more concrete and convincing way in my recent book, *In the beginning . . . Creativity*, I discovered that a radically different way of thinking about Jesus was now also required. And that led to the writing of the present book—a far cry from what I would have written in 1976.

I am deeply indebted to five persons who made important contributions to this book. Dr. Adele Anderson strongly supported this project from its very beginning; she and Professor Jennifer Jesse read an early version of the manuscript in its entirety and made important suggestions on how to improve it. Professor Karen King read chapter 1 with care, helped me formulate more accurately some of my biblical interpretations, and saved me from making a number of serious mistakes. I am very grateful to Michael West, editor-in-chief, for many suggestions clarifying obscurities in the text and making sure that possible misunderstandings are avoided. I am also grateful to my son, Dr. David W. Kaufman, who got me out of a good many computer jams.

chapter one

Reconceiving the Jesus-Trajectory

From the very beginning of Christian faith, it was taken for granted that *God* was the ultimate point of reference in terms of which all human life—indeed, all reality—was to be understood. Christianity emerged initially within the context of first-century Judaism, a religious culture oriented and devoted to the God believed to be the creator of the world and its ongoing ruler and governor, as emphasized throughout the Hebrew Bible:

> I am Yahweh, and there is no other.
> I form light and create darkness,
> I make weal and create woe,
> I am Yahweh, who do all these things. . . .
>
> I made the earth,
> and created man upon it;
> it was my hands that stretched out the heavens,
> and I commanded all their host. (Isa. 45:6b-7, 12 RSV)

It was in this monotheistic religio-cultural context that Christian faith was born. Monotheistic religious orientations, as I have argued elsewhere (Kaufman 1993:ch. 6), tend to generate a three-dimensional world-picture: *God* is the ultimate reality in terms of which all else is to be understood; *humanity* is that self-conscious, confused, and inquisitive creation of God whose conflicted ongoing story—particularly in relation to God—is rehearsed, meditated on, scrutinized, interpreted, assessed, and revised; and *the world* is the overarching context within which this human life, with all its troubles, struggles, and triumphs, transpires. Christian faith, however—though born within this religio-cultural context, and understanding itself as a continuing monotheistic religious orientation—is *four*-dimensional: in its world-picture *Jesus Christ* is as indispensable a dimension as the other three.[1]

From an early period it was maintained by at least some Christians (as the New Testament shows) that Jesus is of absolutely decisive significance for understanding both who or what God is and what human life is all about. Jesus was said to be, on the one hand, the definitive revelation of God, the very "image of the invisible God," as Colossians 1:15 puts it.[2] On the other hand, it was claimed that Jesus is utterly human: "made like his brethren in every respect," as Hebrews 2:17 (RSV) declares, and the very model of human perfection, "tempted as we are, yet without sinning" (4:15 RSV). This double significance of Christ was given dogmatic definition at the Council of Chalcedon (451 c.e.), where it was affirmed that Jesus was "perfect in Godhead ... [and] perfect in humanness, truly God and truly human, ... consubstantial with the Father in Godhead, and ... consubstantial with us in humanness, ... two natures ... in one Person" (Hardy 1954:373, slightly altered). If our task here were to understand correctly the history of christology, we would, of course, have to puzzle out the meanings of all this quasi-mythical language; and that would be a long and complicated assignment.[3] In my opinion, however, Christian theology should no longer be thought of as essentially a hermeneutical task, that is, as largely interpretation of traditional material. Although one cannot do theology properly without awareness and understanding of the main Christian traditions, its central task is essentially *constructive*: to put together a Christian world-picture (or some important features of that picture) appropriate, in a specific context, for orienting human life, reflection, and devotion. We cannot carry out this task, of course, without paying serious attention to the traditions that have informed Christian faith in the past. However, in the course of history, from the time of Jesus up to the present, great changes in and many variations of Christian faith and life have appeared, as Christians have had to adapt themselves repeatedly to new unforeseen circumstances. So our theological task today is to construct a Christian world-picture that can orient faith and life appropriately and effectively in today's rapidly changing modern/postmodern world.

I

In my recent book, *In the beginning* . . . *Creativity* (Kaufman 2004), I suggested that in our world today the traditional defining notion of God as The Creator has become for many virtually unintelligible; and I suggested that such persons might, therefore, think of God simply as *creativity* (a descendant of that traditional idea).[4] What does it mean to place our faith in God-as-creativity? And what does it mean to order our activities, lives, and worship in relation to God as so conceived? For monotheistic believers in our time, in my opinion, it is meaningful and helpful to think of *creativity* as the ultimate point of reference in terms of which life should be oriented; and in that book, therefore, it was argued that it is appropriate, in the widespread ordinary employment of the name God, to understand that it is creativity to which that name refers. Because the focus in that book was on these quite general concerns, very little was said there about Christian faith's other major symbol, Jesus Christ.[5] In the present book, however, I develop—in close connection with my proposal that we think of God as creativity—an interpretation of the correlative importance of Jesus, for those who wish to understand this creativity from a Christian point of view.

Before turning to that, we need to take note of some implications of the traditional understanding of God as the creator of the heavens and the earth, the creator of all things visible and invisible. The mark that came to distinguish God decisively from everything else was, as these phrases imply, *creativity*: everything other than God was created by God; God alone had self-existence, *aseity*. God was not thought of only as creator, however. Before the Israelites came to believe that their god Yahweh was creator of everything, they had known him[6] as a mighty warrior (who brought the children of Israel out of Egypt and who overpowered the Canaanites, giving their land to the Israelites); and he was also a lawgiver, ruler, judge, and so on. All of these roles helped to fill in the picture of God as an almighty but nevertheless humanlike, male-gendered being. This thoroughly *anthropomorphic* conception of God had clear implications for the way in which men and women should live: they were expected to obey faithfully God's commandments and his ongoing guidance (as loyal subjects of a good king would do); and they were expected to manifest grateful, loving, and worshipful responses to God's glorious presence (as the recipients of a great benefactor's largesse should do); and so on. These matters were not just general admonitions: their meaning was spelled out in detail in the legal sections of the Pentateuch (the first five books of the Bible), and faithful Israelites (as well as, later on, their Jewish descendants) sought to order their lives in accord with these detailed holy prescriptions. By keeping the Torah (those teachings given the Israelites by God) in focus, they would order their lives in accord with God's will and would thus be oriented properly in the world. Only gradually, as the glory of the Israelite God was increasingly magnified in the consciousness and devotion of his worshipers, did he become understood as the creator of all that existed. So at the time the Hebrew Bible was put together and creativity had come to be the defining mark that distinguished God from all else, he was also believed to be active in, and supervisory over, the lives of his devotees in many respects. Humans have always had laws, ideals, institutions, hopes and expectations, ways of living and ordering life socially, politically, economically, and so on; in ancient Israel it was believed that all of these had been given by God, and they were to be obeyed as such. So God was not only the creator. God was also a ruler and mighty warrior, a lawgiver and judge (all humanlike characterizations). And God was the Holy One, source of all meaning and value. God was actively involved in the everyday life of the Hebrew people with whom he had made a covenant and to whom he had given the Torah.

With the emergence of Christianity, however—especially as it became a largely Gentile movement in the work of the apostle Paul and others, and moved beyond its Jewish origins—much of this orientation of life in terms defined by the Torah was changed, as the Christian gospel (the "good news" about Jesus Christ) supplanted Jewish circumcision and purity laws.[7] The basic conception of God as the creator of the world was retained (although there was a considerable struggle in the

early church about that matter), but the principal focus for the ongoing everyday ordering and orienting of human life became Jesus the
Christ:[8] his proclamation of the impending "reign of God"; his ministry
of healing and caring for those whom others despised; his inclusive meal
practices; his radical insistence on love for, forgiveness of, and reconciliation with not only one's friends and neighbors but one's enemies as well;
his mysterious "appearances" to his disciples and others after his death.
Jesus was obviously a very remarkable, charismatic figure, and it should
not surprise us that what he lived and taught and endured filled the
imaginations of his small group of close followers with memories and
hopes, ideals and dreams of quite new possibilities for women and men.
Ongoing Christian existence—discipleship to Jesus—involved a new
transformed life oriented in terms drawn from the (developing) story
and image of Jesus, whom Christians regarded as their *Lord* and whom
they believed would soon be seen by all to be the Lord of the world, the
Son of God, indeed the very incarnation of God on earth. As Paul put
it in one of his early letters (drawing on what are thought to have been
words of an older Christian hymn):

> Let the same mind be in you that was in Christ Jesus, who,
> though he was in the form of God, did not regard equality with
> God as something to be exploited, but emptied himself, taking
> the form of a slave, being born in human likeness. And being
> found in human form, he humbled himself and became obedient
> to the point of death—even death on a cross. Therefore God
> also highly exalted him and gave him the name that is above
> every name, so that at the name of Jesus every knee should bend,
> in heaven and on earth and under the earth, and every tongue
> should confess that Jesus Christ is Lord, to the glory of God the
> Father. (Phil. 2:5-11)

Thus, the early Christians came to understand their living relation to God the creator as mediated to them in a decisively new and
distinctive way: through Jesus Christ their Lord, the very Son of God.
In this new situation, obedience to the elaborate legal prescriptions of
the Torah no longer provided proper orientation in life and the world;
God's action in and through Jesus (that is, through the continuously

developing image and story of Jesus) now provided the focus and frame of orientation for life on earth: the followers of Jesus were to take up ministries of reconciliation through which God was "reconciling the world to himself" (2 Cor. 5:19).

In the early Christian movement Jesus was understood in a number of quite different ways, some of these very different from Paul's views just cited. All of these, however, were expressed and formulated in what we today must regard as *anthropomorphic* (humanlike) ideas of God and the relation of God to humans. In this book (as well as in other writings of mine) these anthropomorphic ideas are displaced by the understanding of God as simply *creativity* (instead of a humanlike person thought of as The Creator). Thus, God will be regarded here as that utterly amazing mystery of serendipitous creativity manifest throughout the universe from the Big Bang onward, first in cosmic and biological evolutionary developments, and then ultimately producing—in part through the emergence of *human* creative activity—the human world of history, culture, highly complex levels of symbolization, and elaborate technologies. When we take up this standpoint, it is no longer appropriate to think in terms of the earlier anthropomorphic conceptions. And it becomes necessary, therefore, to reconsider the entire traditional christological development and understanding, conceiving it now in terms appropriate to the conception of God as creativity.

II

However awe-inspiring and beautiful the modern/postmodern story of the steadily developing creation of the universe may be, the notion of creativity by itself—like the notion of God the creator by itself—is not sufficient for developing a conception of God that can fully and adequately orient and order human life. In Judaism, as we have observed, God's Torah provides central guidance on how life is to be ordered; in Islam similarly there is the Qur'an, also thought of as provided by God. And in Christianity there has been Jesus Christ—not a body of prescriptions and laws, but a human being who came to be thought of as the very incarnation of God on earth. These "additions"—going beyond God's fundamental relation to humans (as creator)—were indispensable for the orienting and ordering of life. Creativity, as we will be thinking of it here, is that to which everything that exists is attributed—whether massive or infinitesimal, material or ideal, beautiful or ugly, valuable or useless, meaningful or meaningless, good or evil, true or false, and on and on. (The negative character of some of the items in this list will be discussed in a moment.) It is important to note that reference to creativity does not explain *why* things exist: "creativity" is simply the *name*—not the explanation—of an ultimate mystery that we humans have never been able to put aside and likely will never adequately understand: Why is there something, not nothing? Why does anything at all exist? Why has this amazing phantasmagoria we call the world come into being? The bare conception of creativity does not itself give us answers to any of these questions. It simply affirms that everything in this vast magnificent universe, so far as we know, has somehow *come into being* and therefore *exists*, and it may continue to exist for an indefinite period of time; but in no way does creativity explain why or how that has happened. Creativity—the coming into being of new realities—is an inscrutable mystery.[9] In this respect it may seem to differ from the creative activity ascribed to the creator-God: God was thought of (anthropomorphically) as *deciding* to create this and that and *then performing the act* of creating, of bringing into being the new. That may seem to provide an answer to our question about why things exist. However, if one reflects on this matter, it will become clear that this act of God creating everything "from nothing" is no less a mystery than is bare creativity: we do not have any more *knowledge* about the activities of "the creator" (we have only the biblical legends) than we do of bare creativity.[10]

Since creativity is utter mystery to us, it cannot provide much guidance on most of the issues with which we must come to terms as we seek to orient and order our lives. For that we need stories and images, norms and standards and laws, values and meanings and criteria much more specific and definite. For Christians, from the earliest generations on, such guidance and inspiration has been found (as was just noted) in the lordship of Jesus Christ. If Christians today still find themselves looking to the image and story of Jesus for such significant orientation, it is because Jesus, like Socrates or the Buddha, impresses some men and women even today as a remarkable, in certain respects very attractive, indeed a charismatic figure, one who may still draw us to himself in a

Note: GK is more agnostic than I wish to be. I want to say that God as creativity is ground partly by faith a la p.?

powerful way (as he did the earliest Christians and many others over the past two thousand years). Before we turn to that, however, we need to take note of an important respect in which the mystery of creativity—God—does directly provide a somewhat vague and general but important kind of orientation for human living and acting.[11]

There is a definite qualitative distinction between God and all the creatures—between creativity and everything created. This distinction is the basis for regarding God as, in the last analysis, the only appropriate focus for human devotion and worship. All other realities, being created goods that come into being and pass away, become dangerous idols that can bring disaster into human affairs when worshiped and made the central focus of human orientation. So it is the *mystery* of creativity (God) to which we must turn when we seek an *overall* orientation in life. To attempt to order our lives with this important distinction between God and the idols in mind can only be, of course, a move of faith, of a deep trust in this mystery that has brought us into being and continues to sustain us. We humans—as beings that have emerged on one of the countless creative trajectories moving through the cosmos—are indissolubly part of the *created* order and (despite our own creative powers) not in any way to be confused with the mystery of creativity manifest throughout the cosmos, in all its complexity, order, and beauty. We can exist only (as far as we are aware) within the boundaries and conditions of life found on the particular trajectory in the created order within which we have emerged.

This suggests that we humans should always seek to live and act in *response* to the creativity going on in the world roundabout us and in our lives; for if we do not so live and act, we will soon be out of tune and out of touch with what is really happening in the world. H. Richard Niebuhr put the point well:

> To discern the ways of God not in supernatural but in all natural and historic events, to respond to his intention present in and beyond and through all finite intentions, that is the way of responsibility to God. It is a way of universal responsibility because there is no action in the whole extent of actuality in which the universal intention, the meaning of the One beyond the many, is not present. (Niebuhr 1963:170)

The pertinence of this notion to our concerns here—though it is expressed in anthropomorphic terms (God's "intention")—is obvious: we should always seek to respond to the *creativity* that is manifest *in the situation* in which we find ourselves, creativity in the natural order as well as the historical orders within which we are living. But how does one discern what is truly creative in this complex world of events and actions? This will, of course, always be a judgment call in which we could be mistaken. (That is also the case with Niebuhr's more anthropomorphic formulation.) We should seek this creativity (God) not only in programs and projects to which we ourselves are committed but also in activities and events about which we are inclined to be very critical or even contemptuous. For it may be only as we open ourselves to the serendipitous creativity manifest in events and movements alien to our inclinations that we will come to deeper discernment of what is really going on in our world, and thus be enabled to respond creatively to this divine creativity instead of falling into idolatries of one sort or another. We can desire and hope, thus, that our activities and projects—our *human* creativity—will become blended into the creativity going on in the world roundabout us. In this very important overarching respect, loyalty to God, the mystery of creativity, and faith in this ultimate mystery provide an indispensable dimension to our orientation in life and the world.

III

As we have noted, beginning with the early period immediately after Jesus' death and "resurrection" and continuing all the way down to the present, Christians have viewed God in light of the overpowering significance (to them) of the figure of Jesus. (I put quotation marks around the word "resurrection" here because of its highly problematic meaning now to be discussed.) Our understanding of God as creativity instead of as The Creator—that is, our nonanthropomorphic and nonanthropocentric understanding—requires that we note right away that the idea of resurrection is in question. Most contemporary historians studying this matter are convinced that it is not possible to understand how the early church came into being apart from some sort of "appearances" of Jesus to his disciples and others after his death, experiences that led them to believe God had resurrected Jesus from the dead.[12]

Some historians may feel it is important to develop "a theory of the resurrection," but that is not necessary for our purposes here. Some quite dramatic events apparently occurred that rejuvenated, transformed, and reignited the faith of the followers of Jesus after his death. And the important point for our purposes is that these events (as we shall see) had enormously *creative* consequences. Since the words "appearances" of Jesus and "resurrection" of Jesus are the standard terms used in the New Testament to refer to these enigmatic happenings, I too will employ them when referring to these events, whatever they may actually have been.

From early on (probably already during his life) Jesus was regarded by some as God's messiah (God's "anointed one"), who was expected to overcome all earthly rulers and inaugurate the kingdom of God on earth. In his preaching and teaching God's kingship was central;[13] and signs of its imminent coming were seen by Jesus and his followers in his healings, his open table-fellowship, his respect for women, his forgiveness of sins, and other practices. It is important to note, however, that Jesus' view of how God's kingdom would come on earth was very different from the views of those who expected a military revolt against Rome. This apparently did not become clear to his followers until after his death. Jesus' crucifixion was at first an enormous blow to the disciples, but his completely unexpected appearances shortly after the crucifixion convinced (most of?) them that he had "been raised from the dead, the first fruits of those who have died," as Paul put it (1 Cor. 15:20) in the earliest discussion still extant of Jesus' resurrection.[14] This resurrection of Jesus meant that he was chosen by God to bring in the New Age. According to Paul, "Jesus Christ our Lord" was "designated Son of God in power ... by his resurrection from the dead" (Rom. 1:4 RSV); "as all die in Adam, so all will be made alive in Christ.... Then comes the end, when he hands over the kingdom to God the Father, after he has destroyed every ruler and authority and every power" (1 Cor. 15:22, 24). Evidently Jesus was believed by Paul (and many of Jesus' other early followers) to be the central figure through whom God was bringing all the evil in human affairs to a final end, thus completely establishing God's righteous rule.

It is important to note that in the text just cited Paul does not present Jesus as on a level with God, but rather as the central agent through whom God's righteous kingship over all human activities was being established. What I call Jesus-trajectory$_1$—the historically developing elevation of Jesus to fully divine status[15]—is clearly under way here, but it has not yet reached its apex. It is convenient to think of this movement into deity as consisting of four distinct conceptual steps. (Doubtless it could be broken down in other ways.) The first step begins with Jesus' public baptism; continues through his ministry of preaching and teaching about the coming kingdom of God, performing healings of many sorts, and showing in other ways that a New Age is at hand; and finally culminates in his crucifixion.[16] A second step is the emergence (after his crucifixion) of his followers' belief that Jesus had been raised from the dead and had appeared to them, thus becoming seen as the "Son of God" and their "Lord," about to bring in God's kingdom. A third conceptual step in this trajectory is the emergence of the conviction that Jesus had been elevated to heaven and that his life on earth was actually the very incarnation of God on earth, a claim clearly made in the text of the Fourth Gospel (written many years later than Paul's writings earlier quoted). In the Johannine text it is explicitly declared that the "Word" that "was God" (John 1:1), the Word through which "all things came into being" (1:3), this Word "became flesh and lived among us [as Jesus], and we have seen his glory" (1:14). The Johannine Jesus himself declared that "the Father and I are one" (10:30); and this became a central conviction, as the followers of Jesus who had continued to express doubts about him and his resurrection finally became able to proclaim joyously that Jesus was, as the disciple Thomas put it (according to the Fourth Gospel), "my Lord and my God!" (20:28). Finally, the trajectory reaches its apex in the church's development of the doctrine of the trinity, in which it is officially stated that God is a reality with "one nature" in "three persons"—Father, Son (Jesus Christ), and Holy Spirit—all of equal divine status.[17]

We now have before us an outline of Jesus-trajectory$_1$ as found in the New Testament and early Christian doctrinal history.[18] With the doctrine of the trinity, Christians were trying to make it clear that they did not think of themselves as worshiping two (or three) gods, even though the phrases "God the Father" and "God the Son" seem to designate two different realities. From early on, as we have seen, God had come to be thought of as creator of all that is—and it was this that distinguished God decisively from everything else (regarded as creatures, realities created by God). This was, of course (as we noted), an incomplete characterization of God: for the early Israelites God was also thought of as warrior, ruler, judge, lawgiver, and so on; and without God's gift of the Torah they would not have been able to orient themselves in accord with the divine will (which was hidden and inaccessible, a mystery). For Jesus' followers, however, the overpowering impact of his ministry, death, and resurrection—at first only on a small group of Jewish women and men, then in succeeding decades becoming a largely Gentile movement—changed all of this decisively, as Jesus-trajectory$_1$ gradually became clear (i.e., was created). Jesus Christ became the lens through which the creator-God was now increasingly seen; the image of the crucified messiah and his resurrection put everything in a dramatic new light, as the exalted rhetoric of a variety of New Testament authors shows clearly:

+ "No one knows the Father except the Son and anyone to whom the Son chooses to reveal him" (Matt. 11:27). Here the hiddenness or invisibility of God is asserted, together with the exclusive revelation of God through Christ. According to Matthew, this claim was made by Jesus himself.

+ "No one has ever seen God; the only Son, who is in the bosom of the Father, he has made him known" (John 1:18 RSV). Again, God the Father is completely out of the reach of humans; but Jesus "has made him known." In another Johannine text this hiddenness of God is repeated, and its implications for human life are stated: "No one has ever seen God; if we love one another, God lives in us, and his love is perfected in us" (1 John 4:12).

+ "He is the image of the invisible God" (Col. 1:15). Here again, apart from Jesus Christ, God the creator is "invisible": inaccessible to human perception, experience, knowledge. In the next verse, this connection of Christ with the creator is reinforced further by the declaration that he was actually God's agent in creation: "In him all things in heaven and on earth were created" (1:16), a claim also made (as we have seen) in the Fourth Gospel (John 1:3).

+ "The Father and I are one" (John 10:30). Here we have a full unity of Jesus and God, also put in Jesus' mouth.

This is remarkably strong language: it claims that God had actually been basically inaccessible to men and women through most of human history, but had become accessible through Jesus, that is, through the complex of events surrounding and following upon the ministry and death of Jesus. Surely these writers must have been aware that Jews knew about and had been worshiping this very God for centuries, and that in fact it was from Jews that Gentile Christians learned about God in the first place. Some Christians, such as Marcion—being thoroughly convinced that what was revealed in Jesus was radically different from what was known of the Jewish God—went so far as to insist that Jesus had revealed a new and true God, a God who was not the creator of the present world at all. Obviously these texts just cited were written by persons who believed that a dramatically new connectedness with the Jewish God had come to humankind in and through Jesus, and that apart from Jesus, no one really can know who or what God is and what God requires of us humans. That is, apart from Jesus, God is ultimately inscrutable mystery—a mystery that had, however, been unveiled in and through the person, life, death, and resurrection of Jesus.[19] The Jewishness of Christian faith must have been known and admitted by most early Christians, but the growing sense of the revelatory and salvific importance of *Jesus* eventually led to the conviction, widespread in the churches, that he was himself divine—one with God the Father (and thus of much greater authority than Moses or any other prophet). During the earliest Christian centuries, however, there were a good many followers who did not make these extravagant claims culminating in the doctrine of the trinity; ultimately those Christians did not prevail.

This meant, then, that for many Christians the God who was creator of the heavens and the earth had in some sense deliberately entered into human history in and through the man Jesus. The God who created the world and ruled it from on high had somehow made himself incarnate. This mix of mythical and historical thinking must have been very puzzling, perhaps barely intelligible to many thoughtful persons; and throughout the early centuries the churches had to struggle to make sense of it. The creeds produced at two important councils of church bishops—in Nicea in 325 and Chalcedon in 451[20]—have been regarded in most churches as the authoritative statements about how the complex relationship between Jesus and the creator-God was to be understood. These formulations are very ambiguous and difficult, and to some persons simply incredible or even unintelligible. In any case, however, the project we are undertaking in this book undermines central assumptions of the anthropomorphic language in which these credal formulations were expressed, so we need not pursue those problems further here.

IV

The conception of God (as I have been pointing out), which all Christian parties in these theological discussions and debates appear to have taken for granted, is anthropomorphic and anthropocentric through and through. God's resemblance to humans is very deep: God is conceived as basically like a human agent, although much more powerful in all respects than any human. It is a "God Who Acts" (as G. Ernest Wright put it in a book by that name published many years ago [Wright 1952]). Thus, God has plans, makes decisions, performs actions to carry out those decisions, sometimes decides to change course and move in a different direction. God is fundamentally an *agent* engaged in *doing things*. All of this is clearly modeled on human agency. God also has feelings of many different sorts, such as anger, joy, hatred, and love; God has goals and is working to achieve these goals; God speaks and otherwise communicates; and so on. As we have noted, God was thought of as a mighty warrior, a lord or king, a lawgiver, a judge, a father (who in the Christian story has a son), all of these being humanlike characteristics. This is clearly a thoroughly anthropomorphic God. Even the characteristic that most decisively distinguishes God from everything else—*creativity*—is modeled, in its vivid presentation in the opening chapters of the Bible, on human examples: in Genesis 2 (the earlier text) God is presented as like a potter or sculptor, taking clay from the ground and forming Adam out of it; in Genesis 1 (a later text) God creates by verbal command like a king or military officer: "'Let there be light;' and there was light."

Moreover, this God appears to be concerned largely with human affairs on planet Earth—an *anthropocentrism* also clearly visible throughout the Bible. And it all comes to a crescendo in the Christian story, where it is claimed that "God so loved the world that he gave his only Son, so that everyone who believes in him may not perish but may have eternal life" (John 3:16)—a very powerful, precious, but strongly anthropomorphic and anthropocentric image, one so exaggerated as to suggest that the principal focus of God's activities is the plight of human beings. Many other examples of this thoroughly human-centered character of early Christian thinking about God and God's *agapeic* love for humankind could easily be cited, for this is at the center of the traditional Christian story. The very idea of the incarnation—of God acting self-sacrificially to enter human history in a special way—presupposes both the anthropomorphic notion of an agent-God and the anthropocentric notion of God's *special love* for humankind.[21] And the story of Jesus being resurrected after his death suggests a highly dramatic intervention of God into the human world, an act (both anthropomorphic and anthropocentric) that his followers believed certified not only their claims about the divine authorization of Jesus' ministry, death, and resurrection but also their claims about God's elevation of Jesus into virtual deity. Because of Jesus' obedience to God's will, as the early Christian hymn quoted above tells us, "God ... highly exalted him and gave him the name that is above every name, so that at the name of Jesus every knee should bend, in heaven and on earth and under the earth, and every tongue should confess that Jesus Christ is Lord, to the glory of God the Father" (Phil. 2:9-11).

In my book *In Face of Mystery* (Kaufman 1993), I contend that such a humanlike God—however comprehensible and meaningful it may have been in past generations—is for many, including myself, simply no longer intelligible. And I suggest, therefore, that such persons should cease thinking of God as basically The Creator of the heavens and the earth (a kind of person-agent) and instead begin thinking of God as the *mystery of creativity*, manifest throughout the universe.[22] This creativity—believed to begin with the Big Bang and manifest also in the subsequent cosmic evolution, and later the evolution of life on planet Earth—has ordinarily not been thought of as a kind of deliberate activity of a self-conscious being: it is, rather, a profound mystery. In this modern cosmic picture, to the best of our knowledge, *self-conscious* creative activity does not appear in the universe before the evolutionary emergence of humankind. In the course of the creation and evolution of cultures, languages, and symbol-systems of many different sorts (over several millennia), our human creativity gradually emerged and eventually became a central instrument of human development, a development that in due course has enabled humans to transform the face of the earth dramatically.[23] It is precisely this overall mystery of creativity (in all its cosmic, biological, and human manifestations), I am suggesting, that we should today think of as God. This notion retains the important traditional defining mark of God—creativity—but discards the anthropomorphism and anthropocentrism of its traditional formulations.

With this change in the understanding of God in mind—from God-the-creator to God-as-creativity—let us return to our reflections on the Jesus-story. This change requires us to construct a version of that story quite different from Jesus-trajectory$_1$. What I call Jesus-trajectory$_2$ is the sequence of creative *historical* events beginning with Jesus' baptism, ministry, death, and resurrection, and then continuing on *creatively* through human history all the way to the present. I cannot present here a full account of that trajectory, but I would like to mention some of the important points that should be considered. Looking back from our twenty-first-century standpoint, we can see that the name Jesus has come to signify an enormously creative moment in human affairs. In saying this, I am not giving expression to a Christian faith-claim about Jesus (though Christians would certainly agree with this point). I am, rather, articulating a very widespread historical judgment. The direct influence of Jesus of Nazareth on other persons, during the quite short span of his ministry up to his crucifixion, was, of course, quite limited. It was only within a relatively small and insignificant corner of the Roman Empire that he was known at all. However, the impact of his life, crucifixion, and what his followers called his resurrection on subsequent history has been phenomenal. Something truly new and significant came into the world in and through Jesus' activities, death, and what followed upon his death. In Jesus-trajectory$_1$ we have an account of the important *conceptual* developments that were occurring during these events—developments that enabled the story of Jesus to spread through wider channels shortly after his death, and to grow and multiply over the centuries in many quite diverse ways. In consequence, today the name Jesus is known almost everywhere in the world. In Jesus-trajectory$_2$ now, that conceptual development (in trajectory$_1$) is taken up as a significant moment in the account of the events that followed upon Jesus' death, but it is understood quite differently. What was claimed by Jesus' early followers to be due to the creator-God's working through Jesus to save humanity from its sins and the other evils of life becomes understood, in the modern historical terms of Jesus-trajectory$_2$, as an expression of the extraordinary creativity of the Jesus-movement as it grew and developed after his death and resurrection.

Since in this case we are not working with an anthropomorphic or anthropocentric conception of God as a conscious deliberative agent, but instead with an understanding of God as the mystery of creativity manifest throughout the cosmos, there is no place in this christology for the trajectory$_1$ explanations and interpretations. This important shift in theological understanding should not be regarded as meaning that all talk of God—in connection with Jesus' significance—must be given up. On the contrary, when we uncover events or processes that we take to be truly new or novel in history, it is appropriate to identify them as *creative*; and this means (for the theological standpoint within which we are work-ing) that we should not hesitate to call *God* to mind as we consider these processes and events and their profound mystery. This does not mean, however, that these events are to be regarded as supernatural: today cre-ative events—including extraordinarily important ones—are understood and interpreted in ordinary historical terms. And the events of Jesus' life, therefore, and the import of his activities and of what followed upon his ministry and death, are all to be presented in these terms.

As just noted, one of the most significant historical outcomes of Jesus' activities, death, and resurrection was his fairly rapid elevation after these events—in the minds of many of his followers—to divine status (Jesus-trajectory$_1$). In Jesus-trajectory$_2$, of course, this develop-ment is understood to indicate that Jesus had become of the highest possible order of significance to his followers; and it was this distinc-tive way in which they publicly proclaimed that significance that led to increasing interest in the Jesus-story throughout the wider world in which the early Christian missionaries were spreading it. That is, the claims of Jesus-trajectory$_1$ began to be accepted far beyond their small creative beginnings, and accepted into an increasingly widespread cre-ative movement—an example of the *serendipitous* character that creativ-ity sometimes manifests. It should be obvious that this series of events, which proved to be so highly creative back in the early period when they occurred, would likely not have been regarded as significantly creative at all had they occurred in certain other quite different contexts—for example, in today's modern/postmodern world. Creativity in history is definitely context-relative.[24] This does not mean, however, that these events—accented as creative in Jesus-trajectory$_2$—are not really historical expressions of *Jesus'* creativity; it means, rather, that the historical consequences of Jesus' activities and fate have been extraordinarily complex, and they extend all the way down to the present.[25]

Creativity is always a profound, inexplicable mystery to us humans, something we find difficult—even impossible—to account for: a new transformative reality has unexpectedly appeared; the coming into being of something truly novel has occurred. The creativity in an event or process may not be visible to us as it is happening, and whether it has been creative of good or of ills can be adjudged only as we look back on it: think of the creativity of the American Declaration of Independence; think of the writing of Hitler's *Mein Kampf*; think of the signing of the Magna Carta; think of the Versailles Treaty; think of the Lisbon earthquake; think of the remarkable interpretations of Jesus' crucifixion. Although many creative historical events prove beneficial for humankind and may be seen by some as quite serendipitous, not all powerfully creative events have what we humans call "good outcomes" (as some of the examples just given show). Most creative events are ambiguous in their consequences (from our human point of view). Moreover, the judgments of humans (from significantly different standpoints) about the goodness or evil of certain creative moments in history may be quite diverse and may change over time: consider, for example, the far-reaching creative consequences of the European invasion of the Americas—as seen from the Euro-American point of view and as seen from the perspective of the indigenous peoples. The notion of creativity (God) with which we are working is very widely inclusive; it needs to be nuanced and qualified in ways not yet entirely clear. We will try to work through this complicated matter in some detail in chapter 2.

For the early followers of Jesus, his elevation to divinity through crucifixion and resurrection was believed to be a "mighty act" of God, an act that revealed clearly who Jesus really was, and also revealed God's deep loving care for human beings. As we have seen, this reading of what happened (as in Jesus-trajectory$_1$) is no longer plausible for many today, including many Christians. Does that mean, then, that these events reveal nothing particularly significant to us today? No, not at all. In the theological standpoint with which we are working, God is regarded as *creativity*; and long-extended historical creativity is apparent in these events, as Jesus-trajectory$_2$ clearly shows. This striking creativity will be taken up in more detail in our christological reflections in the next chapter. For this christology to be acceptable today, it must include a plausible historical account—as in Jesus-trajectory$_2$—of the beginnings and the development of this creativity, an account in which everything that occurred is understood (1) to have been within the human sphere on planet Earth and (2) to have been implemented (largely) through human agency—in concert, of course, with the serendipity of the divine creativity. In the first century, like today, it was ordinary women and men who were making the judgments about what was going on in their midst, were producing the interpretations of what it meant, and were making the decisions about what they should do in these circumstances. These specifications concerning first-century Christians, of course, are not some new invention of mine: virtually all scholars working on the historical origins of Christianity take it for granted—as they work out their understanding of these developments—that it is with ordinary human beings that they are dealing.

It should be noted—in any construction of Jesus-trajectory$_2$—that the judgment calls of those first-century followers of Jesus may (or may not) have been the best possible that humans could have made about such matters at that time. But these followers were the ones who had experienced what they took to be appearances of Jesus after his death. And it was they who in consequence announced that God had raised him from the dead and who produced the first interpretations of what this meant for humanity at large. Like all human experiences, judgments, interpretations, decisions, actions—however overpowering, useful, significant, valid these may have seemed at that point in time (and indeed have seemed to many succeeding generations), and however magnificently *creative* these human experiences and acts proved to be—there is no good reason to hold that they should not be subject to further examination, criticism, reformulation, or rejection, as further human judgments (further creativity) in new historical situations (such as the twenty-first century) may demand. Although the originary judgments displayed in Jesus-trajectory$_1$ may have served very well those who produced them, and have continued to serve the churches through much of their history, they should not be idolized, as has often happened in the past. When new times, new understandings of the world and of the human place within the world, and important new problems demand attention, new *creative* responses must be sought.

V

I would like now to sum up the point at which we have arrived. Jesus-trajectory$_1$—our account of the conceptually developing Jesus-story, as we see it in biblical and other early material—presupposes an understanding of God as an anthropomorphic quasi-personal agent-creator, working (sometimes miraculously) through historical events to bring the sinful human sphere on earth fully under his sovereignty. For Christians in the twenty-first century who find this story implausible, it is important to develop a reconstructed version of it—for example, Jesus-trajectory$_2$—if we are convinced that Jesus should continue to have a central place in our lives and faith. Two major changes from the cultural-intellectual environment in which the image and story of Jesus originated and developed will guide our reflections as we work out our christology in this book: (1) the rise of history in modernity as a form of *knowledge* of events (not simply anecdotal reporting)—knowledge based on generally accepted criteria, carefully worked-out argumentation, and plausible imaginative construction of what most likely happened at particular times and places; and (2) the quite different conception of God with which we are working here, as the mystery of *creativity* in the cosmos—the ongoing serendipitous creativity manifest throughout this vast universe that began to come into being fourteen billion years ago with the Big Bang.

There is no question today—after two hundred years of concentrated work on "the problem of the historical Jesus"[26]—that it is possible to construct a reasonable (though perhaps somewhat sketchy and brief) historical account of Jesus' baptism, ministry, and death. We have noted certain features of that account in this chapter and have also given some attention to the resurrection of Jesus and his elevation to divine status.

Going beyond most historical accounts, however, I have pointed out what can quite properly be called the developing *creativity* that becomes increasingly evident as we today look at Jesus-trajectory₂. Were it not for this creativity, we would never have heard of Jesus at all. What are we to make of this?

The reconstruction of Jesus' ministry, leading up to his death as a dangerous rabble-rouser in Roman Palestine, is plausible historically and presents us with a Jesus in many respects still quite attractive: his forthright challenge to the conventional religion of his time; his forceful preaching punctuated with striking parables; his beautiful vision of the coming kingdom of God in which the sick are healed, the poor are cared for, and the outcast and despised are welcomed to the dinner table; his radical emphasis on love as the overarching posture within which humans should live out their lives—love of God, love of neighbor, indeed love of enemies; his unwavering conviction that he must not respond violently against those who were forcing upon him the bitter death of crucifixion;[27] his profound hope that God was bringing in a New Age. But what are we to make of the stories of appearances of Jesus to (some of) his followers after his death, and of their developing conviction (Jesus-trajectory₁) that he was God's divine son, now sitting at the right hand of God the Father, almighty maker of heaven and earth? This conviction led in due course to the conclusion (at the Council of Chalcedon, 451 c.e.) that Jesus had "two natures," one divine and the other human, perfectly united and balanced with each other; and that he was, therefore, "perfect in Godhead ... [and] perfect in humanness, truly God and truly human, consubstantial with the Father in Godhead, and ... consubstantial with us in humanness" (Hardy 1954:373). The human imagination is very creative indeed!

I pointed out above that creativity per se—the simple coming into being of the new, anything and everything new—though quite properly regarded as a manifestation of God, should not always be regarded as good for human affairs (consider, for example, the creativity of Adolf Hitler or the Versailles Treaty, or the creation of ugliness and evil). The human story at large has, obviously, many examples of what we men and women cannot but regard as evil creativity. This problem, of God's creative activity bringing forth what (from a human point of view) is evil as well as what is good, is in fact very old and is taken up in the Bible.

In the book of Isaiah, for example, God is presented as saying: "I am the LORD, and there is no other. I form light and create darkness, I make weal and create woe" (45:6-7). Amos is more pointed: "Does evil befall a city," he asks, "unless the LORD has done it?" (3:6 RSV); and Job asks the same question: "Shall we receive good at the hand of God, and shall we not receive evil?" (2:10b RSV). The entirety of the Book of Job and many of the Psalms are concerned with this matter. It is clear that for at least some biblical writers it is not the case that all acts of God (all manifestations of creativity, to use our terminology) can be regarded as either desireable or good *from our human point of view*. Creativity unqualified, therefore—the divine creativity as such—does not provide an adequate model of how we humans should live and what we should be trying to do. The plot thickens.

What kind of qualifications on creativity can we, or should we, make if we are to continue to use it as one of the criteria important for assessing human action? This question will be taken up later at greater length; for now only a few brief remarks can be made. We need to distinguish between (1) abstract cosmic creativity in general—the coming into being of the universe and of all sorts of realities throughout the universe—and (2) those particular instances of creativity that have appeared in and with the emergence of distinctive evolutionary and historical trajectories on planet Earth. Just as the creativity in the Big Bang is a total mystery to us—Why did this come about? Why is there something, not nothing?—so also is the mystery of the evolutionary creativity manifest throughout the cosmos: Why has creativity brought into being particular trajectory A rather than possible trajectory B? Where are these created trajectories going? Some might suppose that the notion of entropy could help us think through some of these questions, but we really do not know much about how entropy and creativity are related to—or are independent of—each other. In any case, if the universe is running down, its climactic ending is so far distant in the future that there is undoubtedly much unforeseeable, inscrutable, indeed unimaginable creativity still to come before the end is at all near. The creativity in cosmic and biological evolution is indeed a vast mystery, a mystery that tells us almost nothing about how we humans should order our lives—except for the important point (noted above) that we should always keep in mind the fact that this is not a human-centered world, and that we need to beware, therefore, of thinking and acting entirely in human-centered terms.

The creativity that is of *direct* and *specific* importance to us here is, of course, that which is going on in our corner of the universe—the creativity that has, for example, produced on planet Earth the trajectory of life (itself also creative, in its own distinctive way); and still closer home, the creative trajectory that has produced mammals, primates, and finally human beings. Each of these is a distinctive creative trajectory, and each is dependent on many other kinds of creative trajectories in the environment that sustain it. So we have networks of creative trajectories on planet Earth, in various ways supporting and also endangering each other. Much mystery remains here, but we are getting closer to some understanding of what is going on in our immediate environment and thus requires our attention. Although we are far from knowing what the future trajectory of human life on planet Earth will be, we are beginning to understand how this living network of creative trajectories on Earth is sustained and how it sustains us humans. And that brings us to a position from which we can begin to make some judgments about what is good creativity and what evil, *at least for us human beings*[28]—but also for the complex living networks in which we are ensconced. These remarks do not give us any final answers to our questions about creativity, but they do enable us to begin to understand the kind of judgments living on Earth requires us humans to make and the kinds of creativity in which we humans need to be engaged. We must, of course, always be open to the possibility that our judgments will be overridden by the more general trajectories of creativity (God) in the wider universe within which we live.

Let us return now to our question about the creativity of the early Christians who thought in terms of the resurrection and deity of Jesus. What in those ancient ideas remains significant for us today, we who understand ourselves to be living in this world of networks of creative activity? Obviously, since we are working here within the constraints of modern historical methods and are thinking in terms of a (nonanthropomorphic and nonanthropocentric) conception of God as *creativity*, these first-century conclusions about Jesus' resurrection and consequent elevation to deity are no longer plausible or appropriate (as we have been noting). They were, nevertheless, very creative: they were a religio-cultural achievement that had enormous effects on subsequent historical developments all the way down to the present, and they can be expected to have continuing significant effects. The first-century Christians were saying (if we may articulate their view in our twenty-first-century language) that the ultimate divine creativity—God—has participated (and continues to participate) in the human sphere in a special way through the ministry, life, death, and resurrection of Jesus; and therefore Jesus became a kind of criterion or model for those Christians of what human life ought to be, a model that the divine creativity made possible. Although the early Christians understood and spoke of this matter largely in mythic terms that modern Christians may no longer find useful or even intelligible, this claim about Jesus' *normativity* in human affairs remains important to most Christians today.

Many Christians continue to think of Jesus' ministry and death— and (at least some of) the practices and beliefs of the early Christian movement—as presenting important standards and models still valid in today's life and activity. They regard such themes as self-giving love (*agape*), forgiveness, nonviolence, generosity, and the like as of continuing (perhaps universal) significance. These concerns have become especially vivid again in face of the horrors we have lived through during the twentieth century and the early years of the twenty-first, horrors that, in many respects, may be harbingers of the situation of future humanity. This, of course, is a human judgment, but one with potentially wide significance. As we have noted, the early followers of Jesus were also making major judgments that would become significantly creative and influential in the future (though they did not describe what they were believing and doing in these humanistic terms). Although the supernatural features of their judgments go far beyond what we today regard as human competence, there is no reason why we Christians should not reaffirm the aspects of those judgments that we find appropriate. Unlike the earliest Christians, however—who believed that Jesus Christ or the creator-God was revealing important matters to them directly from on high—claims of divine authorization for what we humans today say about these (and other) matters no longer have any proper place in our thinking. Such claims presuppose an anthropomorphic God who makes specific "revelations" to devotees. And we today should identify all such claims as unfortunate early manifestations of the kind of arrogance

Christians have too often displayed in face of those with whom they disagreed.[29] So in our reaffirmations today of early Christian stands, we must always make it clear that we are not taking these positions because God (or Jesus, or creativity) has authorized or commanded us so to do; whatever we say about the significance of Jesus for today will be on the basis of our own judgments, and it must be understood as such. Indeed, we recognize there are always other creative options, other voices, that must also be considered.

Our positions and statements will be made in light of what we see going on in our world, on the one hand, and in light of the direction in which we hope and believe the creativity in our human trajectory (God) is today moving, on the other hand. From the point of view with which we are working here, of course, this burden of human responsibility has *always* been involved: each new generation, indeed each individual Christian, has had to *decide* (at least implicitly)—that is, has had to make judgments—about whether to be active followers of Jesus or simply conventional adherents to local Christian customs. Moreover, this was also the case when Christians began to think of Jesus as Son of God, true God of true God, and so on: it was *they*, and not some higher authority,[30] who was making these claims. This is where the responsibility should always be placed in such matters. In the past, unfortunately, Christians all too often let the powerful rhetoric of their claims drive their judgments, and they believed that their rhetoric itself had come from God. But in fact, as I have been arguing here, this was always their own *human* rhetoric, and we should not idolize it in any way. All too often men and women—because of misunderstandings, ignorance, malfeasance, arrogance—seemingly have not been able to avoid making what later generations would call drastic mistakes. That is to be expected of us humans, and we should be grateful that we now no longer need to accept some of the claims our forebears found indisputable. All of this should, of course, make us more humble about what we ourselves have to say. If we can maintain such humility, that will be a significant creative achievement.

As a conclusion to this chapter and transition to the next, five points should be kept in mind. (1) A conception of God as simply the profound mystery of creativity—like a deistic conception of God as simply creator—is, by itself, too vague and general to provide humans with adequate orientation for the many day-to-day decisions and actions that must be made, though it does provide a criterion for identifying idolatry. (2) In early Christianity the attractiveness and power of the images and stories in Jesus-trajectory$_1$ became accepted as model and criterion for both the divine and the human, and were thus regarded as *normative* in the Christian movement. (3) Many Christians today still feel powerfully drawn toward some of these norms and standards for human living, and it is appropriate, therefore, to develop a christology today to fill in and complete the conception of God as creativity. With such a christology we can work out basic *Christian* norms for human life today, and how it should be oriented. (4) This may also help define what proper worship today might be: not simply bowing down in awe before the alleged authority of God or Christ—or, for that matter, before the ultimate mystery of things—nor consisting largely in flights into mystic ecstasy. It should, rather, express itself in loving our neighbors and our enemies as we love ourselves, caring for the hungry and the poor, taking up "the ministry of reconciliation" (2 Cor. 5:18). As the supernaturalism in the Christian story fades away, its radical *ethical* demands come into sharper focus. (5) To the extent that each of our activities draws on our human creativity, there is, perhaps, a basis here for some modest claims about a significant relationship with God (the ultimate mystery of creativity) as manifest in and through this human creative activity. But of course this would be true of virtually any position we might choose to take: every instance of human devotion and action involves a giving of the self in some sort of creativity (as we shall see in chapter 3). The important issue here is not whether union with God (creativity) is possible or actual; it is, rather, the question about which trajectory (or trajectories) in the universe we should seek to be at one with in our journey on planet Earth today. The story of Jesus points us toward a trajectory emphasizing the creation and sustenance of communities of love and freedom, reconciliation and peace. Is this what we choose to identify ourselves with, or do we prefer something else?

chapter two

Christology:
Jesus as Norm

In chapter 1 we identified two significantly different Jesus-trajectories. The first began with the biblical stories of the baptism, ministry, and crucifixion of Jesus; moved on through Jesus' resurrection into his subsequent rapid elevation (in the minds of his followers) to deity; and culminated in the declaration (by church councils) that he was the second person in the divine trinity—a final defining move that many churches and individual Christians down through the centuries have considered to be the only proper way to think of Jesus. The second trajectory— emphasizing Jesus' *creativity*—begins with the modern historical interpretation of Jesus' baptism, ministry, teachings, and death; moves on into the impressive creativity of the developing acclamation of Jesus as divine (Jesus-trajectory$_1$ and its powerful historical effects); and continues in the historical growth and influence—the ongoing creativity—of the Jesus-movement, ultimately culminating in the worldwide Christian religion and its many sorts of christological belief and reflection. Many Christians today continue to understand Jesus largely in terms of his divinity, as presented in trajectory$_1$; however, many modern/postmodern Christians think of him in more humanistic terms like those suggested by trajectory$_2$. Christians following either of these patterns of interpretation have regarded Jesus as of significant *normative* importance

27

for human beings: normative in the ordering and orientation of their lives, in their thinking about God, and in their expectations concerning the future. It is important now to note that in these two trajectories the *foundation* of the normativity—and hence the normativity itself—is understood in profoundly different ways.

Given the culmination of Jesus-trajectory$_1$ in the conception of God as trinity, with Jesus understood as the fully divine second person of that trinity, his words and actions on earth have often been regarded as the words and actions of God incarnate—to be taken as authoritative revelations of God to humankind. (The resurrected Jesus has also been thought of as continuing to reveal himself occasionally to humans in certain special circumstances, as with Paul's conversion.)[1] Though men and women have interpreted such divine revelations from on high in various ways, for those who think of Jesus largely in the supernatural terms of Jesus-trajectory$_1$, the reports of his words and actions are generally regarded as a kind of absolute truth, to be accepted by faithful Christians without compromise in the ordering and orientation of life. This kind of stance often issues in lives of deep conviction, powerful motivation, and great generosity and self-sacrifice; unfortunately, however, it can also underlie a fundamentalist rigidity and narrowness that is frequently very destructive in human affairs.

In sharp contrast with this understanding of Jesus' significance, when he is understood in terms suggested by Jesus-trajectory$_2$, his normativity takes a quite different shape. Here the dualistic conception of "this world" and some "other world"—of life on earth and life in heaven above, of nature and supernature—is gone, and everything of importance to men and women takes place within the human sphere of life on Earth. This approach, as I am developing it here, does not mean that God is no longer of significance for human life and death: the reality of God—thought of as *creativity*—and the sharp distinction between God and the created order both remain. But this creativity—the ongoing coming into being of the novel and the transformative—is no longer lodged in a person-agent operating on the world from beyond; it is manifest throughout the created order, from the Big Bang all the way down to and including the present.

I

How is the normativity of Jesus to be understood within this second framework? A word needs to be said here about the emergence of norms and standards, values and meanings, in the evolutionary development of human existence on planet Earth. All human cultures have standards and norms of many kinds. Without them, the complex forms of human life that every culture exhibits could never have come into being or continued to exist for long. It took many thousands of years for what we today regard as distinctively *human* life—life including some degree of self-consciousness; the ability to make, and to carry out, deliberate choices about how activities are to be ordered; the ability to take some measure of responsibility for these choices; and so on—to emerge (be created) from a simpler form of animality.

Crucial in this development was the co-evolution of the human brain and our linguistic capabilities, which eventually made possible many diverse forms of symbolic behavior;[2] indeed, the expanding use of linguistic interactions among humans may have been partly responsible for the creation of our large and complex brains.[3] From early on, the biological evolution and the emerging sociocultural historical development of humankind became closely interwoven, and humans became *biohistorical* beings.[4] In chapter 3, we shall see in more detail that as human *symbolic* facility advanced, increasingly complex forms of behavior gradually developed (were created). It was behavior informed, on the one hand, by richer and more detailed remembering and, on the other hand, by the emerging ability to *imagine*—that is, to make present in images and other symbols what is not now being directly experienced. This gradual emergence was, of course, occurring both in individual persons and in the societies and cultures of which they were part. Given these sorts of symbolic/linguistic developments, distinctly different courses of action could be imagined as problems in living came up; and along with this imagining came desires to choose among these alternatives, to make deliberate decisions about what should be done. As this further complexifying and symbolizing—with the growing human imaginative powers—developed in everyday living, a measure of *freedom* was coming on the scene (being created). And to make the choices that were becoming available, it was necessary to have ways to assess the alternatives: values, norms, standards, criteria were required. The human imagination began to create these, and in due course they became central features of the developing cultures: so social mores and eventually formal laws—distinctions between socioculturally approved behavior and what was forbidden—became important dimensions of the cultural traditions to be handed on from generation to generation. The self-consciousness characteristic of our human existence today and the capacity to take responsibility for actions and patterns of living were coming into being (gradually being created) and were beginning to be taken for granted.[5]

Let us return now to the specifically theological issues with which we are here concerned. It is important to recognize that all these developments in the course of the emergence of human biohistorical existence (and many other developments not mentioned) were features of the processes in and through which humanity was being *created*—being brought into being as a distinctly new form of life. Thus, creativity—*God*—was involved at every point along this path. And the profound mystery of this creativity was no doubt beginning to become noticed by (at least some) humans—not only the mystery of these human developments but the mysteries of the surrounding trajectories of life on planet Earth, as well as those in the skies above and the wider universe. Today we can see that in the universe in which we live, creativity seems to be occurring virtually everywhere and in many different ways. From our human perspective, however—with our human time-scales here on Earth—this creativity (God) often seems very slow in its effects, although it occurs sometimes in and through cataclysmic, explosive events.

We humans are products of, as well as participants in, the creative evolutionary trajectory that brought biohistorical forms of life into being, forms of life that have the distinctive powers of imagination, action, and reflection. These emerging powers enabled humans to engage—gradually—in deliberate, self-conscious creativity themselves; and over the last several millenia humans have created many diverse sociocultural worlds as contexts within which to carry on their lives. Our human biohistorical trajectory has not, of course, been an isolated, independent evolutionary development: it is dependent upon, and has been continuously interacting with, many (if not all) of the other evolutionary trajectories in the web of life on Earth; and it could not exist apart from this living ecosystem that brought it into being and continues to sustain it. A major question that confronts us humans today is this: Are we going to find a way to live effectively and fruitfully within the limits placed on us by the ecological order in which we are situated, or will we ignore these constraints and continue our exuberant exercising of the *destructive* potential of our creative powers, ultimately (perhaps) committing species-suicide? Unlike every other form of life that we know, we humans do not simply *occupy* a niche in the ecological order on planet Earth: we alone are *cognitively aware* of the necessity to have an appropriate niche, and of the possibility that we may destroy our niche if we do not take proper care of it. Moreover, only with deliberate participation from us can a niche adequate for our increasingly self-conscious, deliberative form of life be created;[6] the ongoing creativity in the midst of which we live—God—continuously places strong demands of this sort on our human creativity. Will we respond appropriately to them?

With these concerns in mind, let us return to the question about the normativity of Jesus. In Western culture at large (and in many other places around the world) the name Jesus still has an aura of special meaningfulness, and it commands some measure of respect. When confronting a difficult decision, some people continue to ask themselves something like, what would Jesus do? For serious Christians—and also for a good many others who might not identify themselves in this way—the name of Jesus still calls forth a significant image/meaning/norm/value that is regarded as important for the ordering and orienting of at least some dimensions of life. Which dimensions? Here there would be a wide diversity of answers. For some, Jesus comes up only in connection with Sunday church attendance or through linguistic habits of uttering little cries or prayers in moments of sudden terror or great joy ("Jesus Christ!" "Oh, Jesus!"); but the basic ordering of life is carried on largely with reference to other standards and desires. For others, Jesus is more important: in times of thoughtful reflection on and assessment of their lives, Jesus may come to mind as one who is a model of how one ought to live—outgoing and caring for others, thoughtful and kind, patient and self-giving, forgiving others' offenses. The stories of Jesus' behaviors, practices, and sufferings may be remembered at such times: his concern for the poor and the outcast; his healings and forgiveness of sins; his refusal to resist violently (or to avoid) those who eventually crucified him; his forgiveness of his enemies from the cross; his radical teachings about love of neighbor and love of enemies; his call to followers to "deny themselves and take up their cross and follow me" (Mark 8:34).

Why does Jesus come up for some persons in connection with these moments of self-assessment? In part it is probably because of the continuing challenge to them of his unconventional radical teachings about how we humans ought to live. But more than that, I suspect, is involved: in Jesus' ministry and above all in the events leading up to his death on the cross, we are presented with a dramatic image/story of one who appears to have trusted God absolutely, and in consequence was enabled to interact with his fellow humans with love and care and to forgive even the enemies who were bringing about his death. This image and story of the human Jesus, as depicted particularly in the Synoptic Gospels, has a singular power to draw men and women to itself as a model for human life. (In contrast, the picture of the *divine* Jesus in the Fourth Gospel and in Jesus-trajectory$_1$ may diminish for many the normativity of Jesus for ordinary day-to-day life, since that picture raises serious questions about whether it is appropriate to consider Jesus as a viable model for us frail humans.) In our trajectory$_2$ approach, it is not Jesus' supposed otherworldly *authority* (as Son of God, second person of the trinity, and so on) that gives him normative significance (as is often the case with those who think in terms of Jesus-trajectory$_1$). Rather, this thoroughly *human* Jesus provides us with a picture of profound appeal, a picture in terms of which we may be drawn to measure and judge our own humanness and humaneness. No doubt there are many who are not particularly attracted to this human Jesus or who at best may feel quite ambivalent; and some clearly feel repulsed. But for those who find themselves drawn toward him, Jesus' story and teachings may exert a powerful normative significance, a significance that (as we shall see) can be especially appropriate and important for this present age; and he may become a model in terms of which at least some of today's women and men, like many in the past, find themselves assessing their own humanity.

In this understanding of Jesus as a challenging norm for what it means to be human—how we humans ought to live out our lives—no supernatural authority or extrahuman power (of God, of Jesus, or of an impending afterlife) is invoked to compel our attention. And we remain free to turn, if we choose, toward other ways of orienting our lives, other ways of understanding our humanity, other values and meanings. In today's complex pluralistic world many diverse options (some quite trivial, others consequential and all-consuming) demand our attention. The important point to note here is that if we decide to order our lives in terms of the Jesus-model, whether as groups (such as churches and communities and other organizations) or as individuals, it will be *we* who do the deciding, and *we* who take—or fail to take—the steps to carry out that decision. (The same, of course, is true when we decide to look for other standards and criteria for ordering and orienting our lives.) The responsibility for giving—or not giving—the image/story of Jesus a significantly normative place in our lives and actions falls entirely on us.

This has, of course, always been the case, though the particular point I am emphasizing here may not often have been put so sharply in focus, since many in the past have been informed by claims such as Paul's that all faithful Christians have been *predestined* to affirm Christ as their Lord and Savior[7]—a claim strongly reinforced by scriptural models such as Paul's dramatic conversion on the road to Damascus.[8] Given these authoritative ideas and pictures, it is hardly surprising that the full *human* responsibility for the decisions and commitments of men and women to follow Jesus has frequently been played down severely in Christian history; indeed, it was virtually eliminated in the teachings of some churches.[9] The strong convictions about God's omniscience and omnipotence in traditional Christian faith, an understanding of Jesus in the terms specified by Jesus-trajectory$_1$, and strong convictions about the bondage of human sinfulness and the necessity of Christ's atonement if humans are to become at all free[10] often led to a decisive deemphasizing of the ongoing human role in Christian orientations.

In the theological program being sketched here, however, we are not working within terms specified by Jesus-trajectory$_1$ (or any other two-worlds conception). Hence, we are in a position to give a quite positive reading, on the one hand, to the place of human decisions and actions in religious commitments and, on the other hand, to the significance of the *diversity* of human religious and moral options. This enables us to see more clearly the responsibility we take upon ourselves when we make such commitments. Whether the image/story of Jesus is to be—or is *not* to be—the major guide/norm/standard in terms of which we seek to order our lives, it will be our own choice, a choice for which we humans can and must take full responsibility.[11] Moreover, since the entire sociocultural/religious world was largely a human creation over thousands of years (as we have been observing), we humans of today must also assume full responsibility for that. Unfortunately, our human world is a seriously flawed construction, manifesting many severe evils for which we today must take responsibility. This intimate interconnectedness of human action and creativity with human moral, ethical, and religious sociocultural formations and commitments, responsibilities and failures, will be taken up more fully in the next chapter.[12]

We noted above that humans have been created as part of a biohistorical process that gradually emerged in the wider context of evolving life on planet Earth. This process enables—indeed requires—us today to hold ourselves accountable not only for our particular lives and actions but increasingly for the entire sociocultural/religious world that—over many generations—we humans have brought into being. That world is thoroughly pluralistic, and we today must begin to take responsibility for the importance of this *diversity* in the normative frameworks within which we humans conduct our lives, a very difficult assignment indeed. Only in this way will we be living and acting with a proper openness to, as well as accountability for, not only the religious and cultural pluralism of today's human existence but the human future as well. What is required in a commitment to the normative claims of the image/story of Jesus today is not properly understood if it does not take into account this thoroughly pluralistic character of today's global context.[13]

In our time the various cultural streams—each of which, through most of human history, has developed its own independent character and integrity over many millennia—are increasingly interacting with each other as we create a single interconnected worldwide humanity. Although there have been great civilizations and empires for thousands of years, it was not until the twentieth-century development of modern forms of communication and transportation that truly *global* economic, industrial, political, scientific, cultural, social, and religious networks and institutions could be created. The diverse historical streams that heretofore constituted human history are now increasingly becoming interconnected, and in that respect transcended. The dream of One World, a new global culture and civilization, is at hand. And yet nations and other factions around the world do not hesitate to make war instead of finding peaceful ways to settle disputes. We in America, sad to say, are among today's world leaders in these sorts of destructive activities. At this portentous moment,[14] perhaps more than ever before, we need conceptions of the human and visions of history that will facilitate whatever centuries-long movement there has been toward a more responsible ordering of our lives and our world, an ordering in which the integrity and significance of each tradition and community are acknowledged and the welfare and rights of every individual are respected and nurtured. New cultural patterns of association and cooperation must be developed, new institutions must be invented, new ideologies that are at once universalistic and truly pluralistic must be created.

For these sorts of things to happen, a spirit of self-sacrifice for the well-being of all of humanity—indeed the welfare of the whole network of life on planet Earth—is now needed, a spirit that can subdue the instincts for self-preservation and self-defense that so dominate our communal and ethnic, our national and religious, practices and institutions, as well as our personal lives. Just such a spirit of self-giving, love, reconciliation, and the building of community is what the image/story of Jesus and the early Christian communities powerfully present. For those communities and individuals the *defining paradigm*, in terms of which both humanity and God came to be understood, was this image/ story of Jesus and the new communal order of reconciliation, peace, and love that grew up around him and after his death. Even such ideals as justice, order, love, peace, freedom, and the like were not appropriated by the early Christians simply in their conventional meanings: they were, rather, creatively reconceived in light of the vision of the human and the humane that had become visible through the images and stories of Jesus and his followers. In binding themselves to this historical figure and community, Christians nailed down their normative ideas and values in a much more definite and inescapable way than is possible for most humanisms: the image of the truly human and humane became sharper and more specific, and the radicality of the Christian ethic came into full view. Values such as love, self-giving, forgiveness, reconciliation, and peace came into focus and were made concrete in the dramatic image of the life, suffering, and death of the man on the cross and the stories of his persecuted followers. A powerfully evocative appeal in support of heavy moral demands was thus generated.

II

Up to this point in this chapter we have been considering the normative significance of our trajectory$_2$ image/story of Jesus for the orientation and ordering of human life today. This image/story also played a significant role in the way God came to be understood by the early Christians and their successors. God's true character and activities, they believed, had been newly revealed to humans in and through Jesus' activities and teachings, his character and his fate.

It was in the context of first-century c.e. Jewish religion, as we have noted, that Christian faith emerged (was created), and Jesus and all his earliest followers were Jews. The God of this Jewish religion/culture, thus, was the God to whom the earliest Christians were committed: the creator of the heavens and the earth, the Mighty One who brought the Israelites out of Egypt and gave them the land of Canaan, the Lord of all the world whose messiah ("anointed one") would soon be coming, as it was hoped, to overthrow the Roman rulers of Israel and establish God's perfect kingdom throughout the earth. For a time it seemed to some that Jesus might well be that messiah. However, instead of putting together an army to overthrow the Romans, he went around healing people's diseases, forgiving their sins, and preaching the imminent coming of the kingship of God. Apparently he gained a following fairly quickly—perhaps largely because of his success in exorcizing demons—and both the Roman and the Jewish authorities were concerned that he might be about to lead an insurrection. But when they arrested Jesus, he made no effort to resist them. And then he was crucified by Pilate as an insurrectionist who claimed to be "the king of the Jews"—a failed messiah, as all could see. Then came the big surprise: some of his followers began to claim some days later that Jesus had appeared to them several times since his death and burial, and they believed that God had raised him from the dead.

This claim must have been as great a shock to those who believed it as was Jesus' violent execution. How and why had these things happened?

How were they to be understood? What was God doing in and through this resurrection of Jesus? Perhaps Jesus was not a *failed* messiah at all but was instead a very different kind of messiah than anyone had expected. Some remembered that Isaiah had spoken of a "servant" of God who

> was despised and rejected by others; a man of suffering and acquainted with infirmity; . . . he was despised, and we held him of no account. . . . He was oppressed, and he was afflicted, yet he did not open his mouth; like a lamb that is led to the slaughter, . . . he did not open his mouth. . . . The righteous one, my servant, shall make many righteous, and he shall bear their iniquities. Therefore I will allot him a portion with the great, . . . because he poured out himself to death, and was numbered with the transgressors; yet he bore the sin of many, and made intercession for the transgressors. (Isa. 53:3, 7, 11b-12)

Perhaps Jesus was this "suffering servant" through whom God was going to "make many righteous" precisely by his suffering and death. In that case his resurrection from the dead confirmed that he was indeed God's "anointed one," the messiah.

So Jesus' unusual characteristics and actions were likely an expression of his messianic mission. His love for and kindness to the poor, the oppressed, the outcast; his concern for the sick and disabled, his ministry of healing, and his exorcisms of evil spirits and other miracles; his eating and consorting with "sinners" and his freedom from a legalistic view of the Torah; his teachings about love of neighbors and even of enemies: clearly this was a quite different messianic figure than had been expected. He even told his disciples not to resist persons who were harming them (Matt. 5:39), and he made no efforts to lead an insurrection against Rome; moreover, he refused to respond violently to those who arrested him, and he forbade any resistance by his closest followers. If Jesus' actions and teachings were an expression of God's kingship, then the kingdom of God that Jesus claimed was coming soon must be very different from any ever seen on earth.

Though crowds had flocked to hear Jesus and observe him heal people, his peculiar mix of attitudes, teachings, and actions was in many respects confusing. Jesus' followers must have been quite puzzled about what was really going on in and through Jesus' ministry and death. But now after his death, his life and teachings and unresisting acceptance of his crucifixion had all received divine certification by his "resurrection from the dead" (Rom. 1:4; cf. Acts 2:22-24, 32-36). So God's salvation would not involve a military overthrow of Rome; it was coming, instead, through the ministry, death, and resurrection of Jesus. All of this implied that God also must be very different than had been supposed. It took some time for the followers of Jesus to work this out—that is, to create a meaningful interpretation of it—but eventually they were convinced they must say things like this:"No one has ever seen God; the only Son, who is in the bosom of the Father, he has made him known" (John 1:18 RSV)."No one [really] knows the Father except the Son and anyone to whom the Son chooses to reveal him" (Matt. 11:27). "He is the image of the invisible God" (Col. 1:15). The whole understanding of God was now being reconsidered—was being *re-created*—with the image/story of Jesus suggesting a new conception of who God is and how God acts.

The far-reaching character of this transformation in the understanding of God that was under way among the first two or three generations of Christians after Jesus' death can be seen more clearly if we take note briefly of the depiction of God in the Hebrew Bible (the scriptures known and used by Jesus and his followers). There are many conflicting stories and pictures;[15] I can give only a few examples here. The Israelites first became acquainted with God (Yahweh) in connection with their escape under Moses from slavery in Egypt (probably in the thirteenth century B.C.E.). As later generations told the story of that escape, it was emphasized that Yahweh was the mighty"warrior" who made the escape possible, first through sending plagues to decimate the Egyptians and then through overpowering the military forces of Pharaoh by drowning them all in the Red Sea (Exod. 6–12).[16] Eventually Yahweh led the Israelites into Canaan, their new home, and he demanded very brutal treatment of the enemies they conquered in that invasion. During a battle with the Midianites, for example, he commanded them to kill every male and every adult female, saving only the"young girls who have not known a man by sleeping with him" (Num. 31:18). There are many stories in the Old Testament displaying God's bloodthirsty cruelty;[17] and there are many passages in the Psalms and the prophetic and historical writings that celebrate this. When Israelites (and later on Jews) were in political or military trouble, they remembered these grand old stories and hoped God would soon move again to deliver them. It was a "messiah" from God of this sort that—hundreds of years later—many still hoped would be sent to deliver them from Rome.

The God of Israel was not, of course, just a bloodthirsty warrior: from the beginning of the Israelite acquaintance with him through Moses, Yahweh was also a lawgiver; and shortly after the people of Israel had escaped from the Egyptians (as the story has it), he made a covenant with them: "If you obey my voice and keep my covenant," he said through Moses, "you shall be my treasured possession out of all the peoples" (Exod. 19:5). The covenant to be obeyed included the Ten Commandments (a version of which is given in Exod. 20:2-17); in due course, however, God's law was understood to include most of the detailed laws to be found throughout the Torah. In a beautiful passage (which must have been written much later) it is reported that at the time the covenant was made, Yahweh characterized himself as "a God merciful and gracious, slow to anger, and abounding in steadfast love and faithfulness, keeping steadfast love for the thousandth generation, forgiving iniquity and transgression and sin, yet by no means clearing the guilty" (Exod. 34:6-7). God's covenantal promise was to care for the needs of the people of Israel in virtually every respect to "the thousandth generation," and the people were bound to obey God's commandments in full.

Following upon the settlement of Canaan, the understanding of God—and along with it the ongoing creation of God's character as a major feature of Israel's culture[18]—developed in a number of important directions. I will mention only two of them here, both strongly influenced by the prophetic movement that gradually developed especially from the eighth century B.C.E. on. (1) God grew from being simply a tribal god into the all-powerful creator of "the heavens and the earth" and the creator of all life, including humans (Gen. 1:1, 11-12, 20-27; 2:7-9). Thus, the exclusive connection of God's rule and power with the activities of the Israelites eventually developed into Israel's monotheism. This reached its peak, perhaps, in some of Second Isaiah's magnificent poetry, in which, for example, Yahweh is represented as saying:

> Listen to me, O Jacob, and Israel, whom I called:
> I am He; I am the first, and I am the last.

My hand laid the foundation of the earth,
and my right hand spread out the heavens;
when I summon them, they stand at attention. (48:12-13)

I am the first and I am the last;
besides me there is no god. (44:6b)

(2) The moral side of this originally quite parochial and vengeful ruler- and warrior-God also developed in important ways: it became expanded with the realization (at least by the prophet Amos and his followers) that God did not confine his care only to the Israelites, but he was also involved with the other peoples roundabout:

Are you not like the Ethiopians to me,
O people of Israel? says the LORD.
Did I not bring Israel up from the land of Egypt,
and the Philistines from Caphtor
and the Arameans from Kir? (Amos 9:7)

And God's moral sensitivity became deeply enriched as virtues such as justice, mercy, and compassion became emphasized. Consider these beautiful words from three of the "eighth-century prophets":

Hate evil and love good,
and establish justice in the gate;
Let justice roll down like waters,
and righteousness like an everflowing stream. (Amos 5:15a, 24)

When Israel was a child, I loved him,
and out of Egypt I called my son.
The more I called them,
the more they went from me. . . .
Yet it was I who taught Ephraim to walk,
I took them up in my arms;
but they did not know that I healed them.
I led them with cords of human kindness,
with bands of love. . . .

I bent down to them and fed them. . . .
My compassion grows warm and tender.
I will not execute my fierce anger;
    I will not again destroy Ephraim;
for I am God and no mortal,
    the Holy One in your midst,
    and I will not come in wrath. (Hosea 11:1-4, 8b-9)

He has told you, O mortal, what is good;
    and what does the LORD require of you
but to do justice, and to love kindness,
    and to walk humbly with your God? (Micah 6:8)

Thus, Yahweh, the mighty warrior who originally sought bloody revenge against his and Israel's enemies and their gods, the lawgiver who regulated unbendingly the details of the Israelites' lives, was gradually being re-created. He was becoming seen as, on the one hand, the all-powerful creator and ruler of the universe, the only God there is and, on the other hand, a compassionate parent who loves and cares for his children. He loves especially the Israelites, of course, with whom he had a covenant, but their neighbors as well. This re-created Yahweh also calls for justice in the land and mercy for the poor and oppressed. In due course this ongoing transformation of the conception of God began to cut deeper. According to the prophet Jeremiah, for example, even the everlasting covenant between God and Israel is to be superseded (a prophecy later believed by early Christians to have been fulfilled with the coming of Jesus):

The days are surely coming, says the LORD, when I will make a new covenant with the house of Israel and the house of Judah. It will not be like the covenant that I made with their ancestors. . . . I will put my law within them, and I will write it on their hearts; and I will be their God, and they shall be my people. No longer shall they teach one another, or say to each other, "Know the LORD," for they shall all know me, from the least of them to the greatest . . . ; for I will forgive their iniquity, and remember their sin no more. (Jer. 31:31-34)

As the moral sensitivity and consciousness of the Hebrews deepened and softened, the vision of who God was and how God behaved was being creatively transformed in more humanizing and humane directions.

Jesus' followers—after his resurrection—continued to think of God as the creator of the world and everything in it; as all-powerful and all-knowing; as loving and merciful and just, and requiring these virtues of humans. However, their understanding of the creator's character and modes of action was changing decisively: the image/story of God's "son" Jesus was becoming the model in terms of which God was increasingly imagined (re-created); and this change has continued to be normative for much Christian thinking about God all the way down to the present. Jesus was clearly not one who exemplified worldly power or who encouraged his disciples' hopes for worldly glory. On the contrary, he is reported to have said:

> "If any want to become my followers, let them deny themselves and take up their cross and follow me. For those who want to save their life will lose it, and those who lose their life for my sake, and for the sake of the gospel, will save it. . . .
>
> "You know that among the Gentiles those whom they recognize as their rulers lord it over them, and their great ones are tyrants over them. But it is not so among you; . . . whoever wishes to be great among you must be your servant, and whoever wishes to be first among you must be slave of all." (Mark 8:34-35; 10:42-44)

Although Mark's Gospel (quoted here) was written about two generations after Jesus' death, and this precise wording likely did not come from Jesus, it clearly represents very pointedly the sort of things he was remembered to have emphasized. Self-aggrandizement had no place: humility, self-giving, and caring for the needs of others were central to his teachings and ministry; and all of this was sealed dramatically with his nonviolent, unresisting acceptance of crucifixion by his enemies.

The community of followers that emerged after Jesus' death understood its mission to be a continuation of Jesus' comportment and work in the world, a continuation of God's creative transformation of humankind that was to culminate in the coming of God's full kingdom on earth. In this community the enlivening presence of God's Spirit was experienced in powerful new ways (cf. Acts 2), and this was transforming the lives of its members. The community they formed is described as one in which "no one claimed private ownership of any possessions, but everything they owned was held in common" (Acts 4:32), and the needy were properly cared for. A generation later Paul was declaring that members of the community were to "walk by the Spirit," seeking to rid themselves of "immorality, . . . idolatry, . . . enmity, strife, jealousy, anger, selfishness, . . . and the like"; and they were to bear "the fruit of the Spirit [which] is love, joy, peace, patience, kindness, goodness, faithfulness, gentleness, self-control" (Gal. 5:16, 19-23 RSV). The transformation that was occurring among them seemed decisive. It was a totally new and fresh start in life. Paul characterized it as a "new *creation*":

> If anyone is in Christ, there is a new creation: everything old has passed away; see, everything has become new! All this is from God, who reconciled us to himself through Christ, and has given us the ministry of reconciliation; that is, in Christ God was reconciling the world to himself, not counting their trespasses against them, and entrusting the message of reconciliation to us. So we are ambassadors for Christ, since God is making his appeal through us. (2 Cor. 5:17-20)

As the Christians had come to believe, God's creative mode of action in the world—God's way of addressing the profound evils in the world—was not in keeping with the expectations of those who had hoped for a military overthrow of Rome by God's messiah. God was a very different sort of reality than they and other Jews had heretofore imagined. They were creating a new picture of God based on and exemplified in the image/story of Jesus (though they probably did not realize this was what they were doing).[19]

This creation of a new image/concept of God was carried furthest in the Johannine writings (toward the end of the first century C.E., or even later). As we have noted, in the Gospel of John the claim is made that Jesus was not just the decisive *revelation* of God; he was in fact *divine*. In the prologue it is made clear that the Word that "was God" and created "all things" (1:1, 3) "became flesh [in Jesus] and lived among us"

(1:14); and later on Jesus is presented as saying forthrightly, "The Father and I are one" (John 10:30). In the First Letter of John the implications of this—both for human life and for the understanding of God—are carefully spelled out:

> Beloved, let us love one another, because love is from God; everyone who loves is born of God and knows God. Whoever does not love does not know God, for *God is love.* God's love was revealed among us in this way: God sent his only Son into the world so that we might live through him. . . . Beloved, since God loved us so much, we also ought to love one another. No one has ever seen God; if we love one another, God lives in us, and his love is perfected in us. . . . *God is love,* and those who abide in love abide in God, and God abides in them. (1 John 4:7-9, 11-12, 16; emphasis added)

It is obvious that we are very far removed here from the "mighty warrior" image in terms of which God was initially introduced to the Israelites. Though that image became tempered and broadened over the following centuries, as we have seen, nothing really approaching this characterization of God as simply and straightforwardly *love* (*agape*) is to be found prior to these Johannine texts. Moreover, a very striking implication of this pronouncement is also drawn here: the writer claims that this understanding of God means that there is one overarching criterion—*love*—in terms of which all human life and activities should be guided and judged, and in terms of which human living in relation to God, the actuality of human faith in God, can be discerned: "Whoever does not love does not know God, for God is love. . . . If we love one another, God lives in us, and his love is perfected in us."

These are very strong claims indeed, transforming significantly even the ontological modality in which God was being imagined; and they are made without qualifications of any kind. Jesus had said that we should love God with all our heart and love our neighbors as we love ourselves (Mark 12:30f) and that we should even love our enemies "so that you may be children of your Father in heaven" (Matt. 5:44-45). And Paul penned a beautiful hymn to love, ranking it above even faith and hope (1 Cor. 13:13). Although these remarks clearly commend love as of central importance to human life, they are far from *identifying* God *as* love. Love was certainly a prominent theme throughout the emerging Christian world, and a member of the Johannine group drew a daring quasi-ontological conclusion from this: it is love that is the ultimate reality with which we humans have to do. Love is not just one of God's qualities; God *is love*—God is an *activity*, not a person.[20]

This was a very important, far-reaching new insight. The point for us to note here is how deeply the image/story of Jesus affected the religious/moral consciousness of at least some of the early Christians, how far they had moved from the understanding of God—and the consequent understanding of human life—that they had inherited. No wonder Paul declared, "If anyone is in Christ, there is a new creation: everything old has passed away" (2 Cor. 5:17). This does not mean that there is no longer any connection to the Jewish past: the basic outline of God as creator and governor of the world remained, along with many other matters; and both Paul and John addressed communities rooted in Judaism as they reflected on the significance of the Jewish figure Jesus.[21] Nor does it mean that all Christians were in agreement about how these changes should be understood. However, during the decades following the death of Jesus, many of his followers seem to have been going through a dramatic "paradigm shift," not only in their conception of themselves and their responsibilities in the world, but in their conception of God as well.

All these developments in the understanding of God—and what God requires of humans—occurred in the first century C.E. in connection with the emergence of Jesus-trajectory$_1$. And it is important that we carry over into Jesus-trajectory$_2$ (in an appropriate way) this aspect of the story that is recounted there: a new and quite distinctive (though still anthropomorphic) way of imagining God, and consequently of humans and their relation to God, was in fact being created—most decisively in the Johannine writings. This new understanding did not completely displace the older anthropomorphic picture, in which God is displayed as having many human moral deficiencies as well as virtues; but it opened up possibilities that would, over the coming centuries, repeatedly stimulate fresh thinking about God. We cannot explore that history here; but it is important that we note the implications of this new understanding as we consider the further extension of Jesus-trajectory$_2$ into today's world. A central question to which we must attend is the pertinence of this new vision for our God-talk today. This Johannine declaration that "God is love" opens the door to thinking of God as a kind of *activity* rather than a person; in that respect it suggests a conception of God similar to that with which we are working in this book (God is *creativity*, not a person-agent).[22]

The Johannine writers do not take up the question of how love might have created the world. But the creation of the world surely could have been imagined as an expression of God as love: in human experience love is at the center of both creative and procreative attitudes and activities, and by extension it might be thought of as having in some way brought forth the universe. For us today, however, this move cannot easily be made for two reasons: (1) As mentioned above, love is itself a thoroughly anthropomorphic concept, and we are attempting here to think of God in nonanthropomorphic terms. (2) The physical world, as we understand it today, could not have been brought into being without massive physical forces, including violent events of many different sorts: exploding stars; cosmic "black holes" that swallow up everything in their vicinity; on planet Earth volcanic eruptions, earthquakes, floods, and so on, and nature "red in tooth and claw"—all of which continue today. This violence appears to be an indispensable feature of the creativity manifest in the cosmos at large. So how can we speak of the creativity (God), which has brought all of this into being, as *love?*

What we can say today is that all of this violence is characteristic of the creative *beginnings* and the ongoing *underpinnings* of a remarkable process in our universe, a process that has included the creation of life, and then much later the creation of agents capable of self-conscious action and (eventually) moral judgments about such matters as violence and nonviolence. This creativity manifest in our universe (God)—in the course of bringing us humans into being—has also brought us to a point where we can entertain the possibility of living in a moral order that is nonviolent and is loving; and we can deliberately choose to work toward such an order. We can educate ourselves and our children to live and act in loving nonviolent ways (however unlikely it may be that the dream of a completely nonviolent human order will ever be fully realized). The emergence of moral values, meanings, and sensitivities—together with the contexts that both require and nourish them—is just as much a product of creativity (God) as are the more ancient material aspects of the universe. Activity, attitudes, and behavior of the sort we call *loving* gradually came into being in and through the processes through which our humanness was being created; and—especially with Jesus and his followers—they came into focus. In due course, in our human corner of the universe, capacities and needs for *agape*-love have gradually become important and prized (at least in some quarters). Thus, in and through our specifically *human* interaction with creativity—with God—loving, caring attitudes and activities have become a significant feature of life. However, this creative development—like many other distinctively human characteristics—came about only in the course of human evolution and history, as far as we know. It is quite unlike what has come into being in the interrelations of creativity (God) with many other spheres of the cosmic order: so the Johannine writer has really gone too far in suggesting that the God of the universe is simply love.

We humans live in worlds of symbols; and this exaggerated Johannine claim does make an important point in that connection. Jesus is, after all, the principal and most dramatic *symbol* humans have of a truly radical ethic of caring, of giving ourselves to others in love. Indeed, it is hard to see how this radical *giving* of our lives for and to others could have become such a powerful idea in our human world without the story of Jesus—that is, without what has been handed down in Jesus-trajectory$_1$. Most people would not even consider such a radical demand; and only a small fraction of those who have thought about it have taken this demand for self-giving seriously. But the image/concept of radical *agape*-love has in fact become an important ideal value to a good many people over the centuries, and for that we have to thank (in part) the pronouncement in 1 John that *God is love*: the ultimate power in the universe is *love*. Down through the centuries Christians have received the symbols of Jesus and love—symbols most powerfully dramatized in Jesus' crucifixion, on the one hand, and in the declaration that *God is love*, on the other—as central to the very meaning of life; and we today who inherit this tradition must decide whether we should still take this insistence on radical love seriously or not. In the last twenty centuries there have always been persons who, upon encountering the figure of Jesus and the emphasis on love, found they had to make a deliberate decision whether to commit themselves to these symbols in a radical way; this has never been an easy decision. And we today also—if we have experienced the powerful attraction of the image/story of Jesus—find we must ponder whether we are willing to orient ourselves and our lives in terms of this vision of the human.

I suggested above that 1 John's insight that "God is love" implies that God is an *activity* rather than a person, and something similar to this is also what I have been suggesting in my proposal that we think of God as *creativity*. For the writer of 1 John, the most important feature of the Jesus-story apparently was that through it God was creating *agape-love* among humans; and he emphasized that point strongly with his declaration: *God is love!* Is that point still so important for us humans that we should continue using this anthropomorphic hyperbole in characterizing God? However beautiful this metaphor is, it expresses—when used without qualification—a thoroughly anthropocentric way of thinking about the creativity manifest throughout the vast cosmos within which we find ourselves, a mistake that I am trying here to correct. What we can say, I think, is something like this: In this book (and in Kaufman 2004) we are exploring the proposal that we think of God as *creativity*, a serendipitous creativity that, in the process of bringing into existence many different forms of being and power, has also created human life; and (as Christians may well believe) in connection with this human life God has—in and with the creativity of Jesus and the early Christian community—created *agape-love* as the central value and norm for orienting and assessing human life and actions.

III

We are now in a position to refine our concept of creativity a bit further. For the most part I have been using this notion in a very broad and general sense: to indicate any example of the bringing into being (or the coming into being) of the novel, of something new—whatever it may be, and wherever and whenever it may be. This characterization may seem to suggest that creativity occurs largely in point-instant events, anywhere and at any time. That would, however, be a misunderstanding: creativity appears most frequently in and through continuous trans-

*creative
trajectories*

formative processes, some very extended—what I have called "creative trajectories" (see, e.g., ch. 1, pp. 22–23). The creativity that followed upon the Big Bang gradually became increasingly specific and distinctive, and in due course quite various. And the creativity in the ensuing evolutionary and historical processes seems always to have involved the coming into being of something new *on a specific trajectory*—a trajectory that had already developed in a particular way that opened it to the possibility of further creative movements in some directions but not in others.[23] In this book we are particularly interested in the creativity manifest in Jesus-trajectory$_2$—that is, the particular historical trajectory that emerged in consequence of the life, ministry, teachings, crucifixion, and resurrection narratives of the man Jesus of Nazareth—a trajectory that has continued to develop and expand in many ways over the subsequent centuries all the way down to the present. We have not yet considered the wider context within which this trajectory itself came into being; and to understand what was involved in that, we must briefly take note of the pattern of creativity that brought Jesus into being.[24] So let us now look backward in time from Jesus, taking note of the complex series of nested creative trajectories from within which he ultimately appeared (was created). We will be in a better position, then, to look forward again to the consequences of his life.

Jesus, as we have been considering him, was a unique historical figure (this general remark can be made, of course, about virtually everyone). He appeared about two thousand years ago in Palestine within what we could call the Hebrew/Jewish *historico-cultural* trajectory, and this was part of a wider complex of historico-cultural trajectories in the eastern Mediterranean region. These trajectories in turn were all aspects of the larger human *biohistorical* trajectory that had its beginnings in Africa, perhaps about five hundred thousand years ago. We could continue, of course, to push this nested pattern of creative developments back through the *biological* trajectories of primates, mammals, and ultimately the beginnings of life on planet Earth, but that is not necessary for our purposes. We have reminded ourselves here of the enormous complexity and longevity of the creativity that brought forth the Middle Eastern historico-cultural trajectories that then provided the context for the appearance of Jesus and for Jesus' life and its consequences.

Most scholars are agreed that the immediate circumstance that brought forth Jesus' ministry was the preaching of John the Baptizer out in the wilderness near the river Jordan. Jesus went to hear John, repented for his sins, was baptized, and became one of John's followers. In due course he, like John, was preaching about the imminent coming of God's kingdom on earth.[25] Jesus, however—quite unlike John, whose hearers had to go out into the wilderness to hear him—wandered from village to village, seeking out people who were despised as sinners and bringing the good news of the coming kingdom of God directly to them (Fredriksen 2000:127–28). Jesus-trajectory$_2$ begins, thus, with a historical account of Jesus' discipleship under John, and then Jesus' own ministry, teachings, death, and subsequent appearances; it proceeds through an account of the enormously creative consequences of Jesus' elevation to deity by his followers (as the Jesus-story of trajectory$_1$ is spread far and wide by Christian missionaries); and then it broadens out in the ongoing history of the various understandings of and commitments to Jesus, down through the ages to the present. Moreover, this trajectory remains open to further creative development.

We need to ask now whether this image/story of Jesus (as presented in Jesus-trajectory$_2$) can inform, in any important way, our understanding of God as creativity. As we have noted, for first-century Christians much of great importance was revealed about God in and through the image/story of Jesus (trajectory$_1$). Does the image/story of Jesus, as we today think about it in connection with trajectory$_2$, reveal anything new about the creativity manifest in our universe (that is, about God)? Some comments, I think, can be made about this. First, consider this example. The emergence of *life* on planet Earth, and eventually of humanity, does say something about the creativity manifest in our universe: in the course of some billions of years (and other necessary conditions), a very complex pattern of creativity developed on planet Earth. It was a creativity that brought into being many different sorts of living creatures (among other things). All of these creatures are, of course, quite complex; some of them—eventually including self-conscious, morally responsible *creative*-creatures, us humans—are extraordinarily complex. If we consider how differently and variously this mode of creativity on planet Earth has produced new forms of life in many quite diverse particular contexts, we can see that it must be enormously *adaptable*—a characteristic not suggested at all by the creativity in the Big Bang.[26] The emergence of life on planet Earth, with its many distinctive species—and later the emergence of *human* life, with its many distinctive societies, cultures, and individuals—does tell us something about the creativity in the universe that we otherwise would not have known.

Every individual person is, of course, a vivid exemplar illustrating these points about the *complexity* of the creativity that has brought humans into being; in this respect, therefore, the emergence of Jesus reveals nothing particularly unique. However, the image/story of Jesus *is* unique in certain very important respects (as we have seen), and this uniqueness must itself be regarded as a manifestation of the creativity on planet Earth (as is every instance of earthly uniqueness). If one believes that the image/story of Jesus presents a kind of definitive picture of what is *normative* for humans—a sense of what human life at its best is all about, a sense of how we ought to live, for what goals we should strive, what is a truly *good* human life and human community—the *distinctiveness* of precisely these norms grounded in this story may quite properly be understood as a unique expression of creativity (God). In this respect, thus, this particular image/story *reveals* something about God (creativity) that we humans otherwise would not know: the divine creativity is involved in the creation of norms by means of which humans can (should?) order their lives.

At first only a very small group of followers discerned that Jesus' life, ministry, teachings, and death had this kind of special importance. And they likely would have missed this point if they had not become convinced that Jesus had been raised from the dead by God and thus certified from on high (Rom. 1:4). With certification like that, however, the Jesus-movement took hold quickly and expanded throughout the Roman Empire and beyond; and in due course the notions of Jesus as unique Son of God, unique second person of the trinity, uniquely definitive revelation of God, and so on, spread around the world.[27] These particular claims, it must be granted, about Jesus' utter uniqueness, or about his being the "image of the invisible God" (Col. 1:15) and the definitive normative model of the human, have always been accepted by some to whom they were presented and refused by others. This last point is very important: only those who accepted the trajectory₁ version of the image/story of Jesus were in a position to regard him as being unique and significant in this special way, as God's only son—and for that reason a new revelation of God's nature and activities. From the beginning on, many others have pooh-poohed this claim, regarding it as ridiculous. And this is also the case today. What are we—with our Jesus-trajectory$_2$ approach—to make of this set of issues inherited from trajectory$_1$ thinking?

As I have suggested repeatedly, creativity—a profound mystery beyond human comprehension—is seemingly involved in virtually everything that happens: large or small, beautiful or ugly, authentic or fake, true or false, good or evil. Can the specific—indeed unique—set of events found in the Jesus-story illuminate in some significant way such an all-encompassing reality as *creativity?*—a creativity in which everything has its origin? Though this wide creativity is the principal criterion (in the theological position sketched here) for identifying the many idolatries into which we humans fall[28]—and that is an important function—the concept of creativity that we have been employing up to this point is too general to provide us with much specific information on anything in particular, and thus any guidance on the decisions and actions, large and small, of everyday life. In Judaism that sort of detailed guidance (as we have seen) was usually provided by the legal sections of the Torah and commentaries on those sections; but in the early decades of the Christian movement, these were largely displaced by the developing image/story of Jesus—his actions and his teachings, his crucifixion and his resurrection—all elaborated and extended in the growing Christian movement as it created Jesus-trajectory$_1$. And in due course this *christic* input into the understanding of God became central to the meaning of the word "God" as it was employed by most Christians: God is a trinity (it was claimed), of which Jesus is the "second person," and God is preeminently *love.* Christianity's inherited monotheism was thus transformed decisively. The image/story of Jesus had revealed a great deal about God that had not been known before. How is all this to be understood in our Jesus-trajectory$_2$ program?

I have been arguing here that God (creativity) must be understood as deeply involved in all aspects of the cosmos, including those that are of little or no significance to us humans; by the same token, of course, creativity (God) must also be seen as intimately involved with us humans, including our deepest longings, commitments, loyalties, loves.

However deeply mysterious is the creativity from which everything has come, included within that "everything" must be the normative dimensions of meaning and value in the human biohistorical trajectory. Creativity (God) must be conceived, thus, to be as intimately and appropriately involved with the dimensions of the human trajectory that make life meaningful and precious as with any others—perhaps more involved in some respects, considering the intricate complexity of these features of the universe. Those respects, then, in which Jesus and love have significant *normative* meaning for Christians are also quite properly to be attributed to creativity (God). The normativity of the image/story of Jesus shows itself in its powerful attractiveness to some men and women as a model for humans, catching their attention and drawing them to itself; and it gives those *who commit themselves to it* a sense of what they can believe God (creativity) is bringing about *on planet Earth*—a sense of the direction in which creativity may be moving in our human world—and (as we may dare to hope) will continue to move in the future. It was, after all, creativity (God) that brought forth Jesus as a normative model, and it was creativity that brought forth love, regarded (by Christians) as the ultimate criterion of what humans ought to become and to be. Because of the openness of *agape*-love to *all comers*—even enemies—there may be some reason to take seriously the Christian claim that love has a certain normative significance for all human existence; and one might make the claim that this particular normativity of love is grounded in nothing less than the divine creativity, the creativity that has produced all humans, has produced our humanness and, indeed, our striving for humaneness.

However important these claims may be for us living on planet Earth, they do not, of course, tell us much about the creativity in the wider cosmos—the creativity that will determine the ultimate future of planet Earth and its inhabitants. We make a mistakenly *anthropocentric* judgment if we think these Christian concerns and activities (all of which are bound up with life on planet Earth) reveal much to us about that wider creativity in the universe at large. The most that the image/story of Jesus may be revealing to us is that the creativity on planet Earth that helped enable human life to emerge, to continue, to flourish, has also helped enable humans to become more loving and humane. And we may well *hope* that future creativity will help us move further down this path. In that very limited way the Jesus image/story may be telling us something very important about what God (creativity) has brought about *in the human trajectory on planet Earth*. All of this, of course, must be considered a matter of (Christian) faith, not knowledge. Faith and hope of this sort can motivate men and women as they seek to live out the paradigm of the human revealed in the story of Jesus and the early Christians. In any case, commitment to Jesus and to *agape*-love, or failure to commit oneself to Jesus and love, is always basically a matter of human consent or decision—or better: it is a matter of the weightiness of a long sequence of historical human decisions and consents, and the deep conviction that this trajectory is a significant expression of the serendipitous creativity we call *God*.

With the notion of Jesus-trajectory$_2$, I am seeking to sketch an alternative to the ministry/death/resurrection/ascension-to-heaven story about Jesus (trajectory$_1$)—an alternative that does not presuppose the outmoded two-worlds framework of the traditional account and that fits into meaningful connection with an understanding of God as creativity. We need now to look at one more important implication of this proposal. The elevation of Jesus to deity (in trajectory$_1$), taken together with the awareness of the presence of the divine Spirit in the life of the Christian communities (see Acts 2; Gal. 5:16—6:1; etc.), made it important for the Christian movement to create an entirely new, previously unheard-of conceptual meaning for the word "trinity": that the "father, son, and holy spirit" are to be understood as *one God*, not three. The concept of trinity that was developed holds these three together in such an indivisible interconnectedness that it is precisely in the solidarity of their *togetherness* (not in their independence from each other) that they are God, the God that Christians have worshiped and served. It is not necessary for our purposes here to spell out the doctrine of the trinity in any detail. I have brought it up because in and through the second motif of the trinitarian concept (the "second person," to use the traditional terminology), the churches have officially declared that Jesus Christ is an indispensable central component of the Christian understanding of God: the second person of the trinity is fully co-equal with the first and third persons in their divine reality. For (most) Christians the image/story of Jesus has been a major ingredient of the meaning of the word "God."

We need to take note here of some problems connected with this idea of God-as-trinity. Given our conception of God-as-creativity, is it appropriate to continue to give this kind of weight to the Jesus image/story? The story of Jesus, in the trajectory$_2$ christology that I have been developing here, is concerned with only one very limited complex of the creativity in the universe: the creativity on planet Earth—more specifically, the creativity in the human biohistorical trajectory on planet Earth. This is a far cry from the traditional trinitarian claim that the three persons of the trinity all co-inhere in each other (the doctrine of *perichoresis*) and are all *equally* involved in everything in which any one of them is involved—and thus equally involved in everything throughout the cosmos. The doctrine of the trinity may be faulted here on two counts: (1) in its lifting a human being (Jesus) up into full deity, it makes the creativity throughout the universe fundamentally *anthropomorphic* and *anthropocentric*; and (2) this sort of move seems to presuppose some version of the old two-worlds cosmology. Hence, for those thinking in terms of something like a Jesus-trajectory$_2$ christology (a move I am proposing for persons who take seriously critical historical methods and modern evolutionary ideas), it is difficult to see how anything like the traditional doctrine of the trinity can still be advocated. Most of the vast universe, as we think of it today, is in no way at all affected by Jesus' life, death, and resurrection; it is only the human project and its evils, on planet Earth, to which the Jesus-story—because of the healing and new life that it has brought—is pertinent.[29]

Some may object to this argument, holding that the idea of trinity is central and indispensable to the Christian understanding of God; and it is not, therefore, a matter of choice or consent for Christian theologians: trinity is simply what God in fact is for Christians. But that is a misleading claim.[30] We need to recognize that from the very beginning of specifically Christian thinking about God, all the major issues that needed addressing involved human *choices*. Doubtless the divine creativity was playing its part in these developments, but from our vantage point today just what that part was remains (as always) a profound mystery. What was visible to the humans participating—and continues to remain visible to us today—were the decisions these humans themselves made. It was through choices made by various followers of Jesus that the affirmations and claims that eventually developed into Jesus-trajectory$_1$

were made; it was the choices of councils of bishops that eventuated in the understanding of what would be regarded as "orthodox" in the churches—including the doctrine of the trinity—and what would be regarded as "heresy"; and it has been repeated choices over the centuries—by bishops and popes, by congregations, by reformers of various sorts as well as other individual women and men—that have determined in every new present whether those earlier choices should still be regarded as of central importance in orienting and ordering life. Choice also determined whether they should be played down to some extent or be completely ignored or be revised and updated. This is, of course, one of the ways in which the ongoing creativity in the historico-cultural process opens up new channels of intellectual development or closes down old ones—in theology as well as in other activities. And so it must also be today, with the doctrine of the trinity as well as other traditional claims. In and through ongoing reflection on the pertinence, or the irrelevance, of the image/story of Jesus for our lives and for today's world, Jesus-trajectory$_2$ continues to develop—or perhaps dies away for us.

IV

We in the twenty-first century are the heirs of many different ways of understanding and interpreting Jesus: Which (if any) should we commit ourselves to and seek to develop further? Which should we ignore or discard? These are difficult questions, and in the past they were often answered on the basis of what was regarded as authoritative divine revelation, an option no longer open to us, as has been argued here. When the churches in the early centuries of Christianity accepted or consented to the notion of orthodoxy, the range of options for Christians was significantly narrowed—though there have always been differences of opinion regarding precisely what "orthodoxy" required, and usually there were some Christians (often called heretics) who chose to reject the dominant orthodoxy. Many different options, thus, have always been available in Christian thinking about God, humanity, Jesus, and the world. And Jesus-trajectory$_2$, as we receive it today, presents us with this variety of interpretations of Christian faith and of the image/story of Jesus. There cannot be any clear, obvious, and universally agreed conclusion about what the uniqueness and significance of the image/story of Jesus consists in. Already in the New Testament period there were strained arguments on this matter between different factions among the followers of Jesus, and this has continued throughout history.[31]

Jesus-trajectory$_2$, thus, actually brings us a number of significantly different Jesuses;[32] to which should we (as groups or as individuals) commit ourselves? Here again we are confronted with a matter of choice or at least consent: Which Jesus, if any, really "grabs" us? Which makes sense to us? Which will help us grow in important new directions? Whatever we regard as of unique significance in the complex of events "surrounding and including and following upon the man Jesus"[33] will largely determine the version of the Jesus-story that we choose as we seek to discern what light that story might throw on human life and death today. In chapter 4 I will take up again this matter of the variety of Jesuses available today and will indicate which of these I find most significant and why.

There is one more important theological issue that must be at least touched upon in this chapter: the traditional Christian belief in an afterlife. On this issue, as on many others, the resurrection of Jesus was determinative in the early church and through much of Christian history. Paul put it this way in a letter to the church in Corinth:

> Now if Christ is proclaimed as raised from the dead, how can some of you say there is no resurrection of the dead? . . . If Christ has not been raised, your faith is futile and you are still in your sins. . . . If for this life only we have hoped in Christ, we are of all people most to be pitied. But in fact Christ has been raised from the dead, the first fruits of those who have died. (1 Cor. 15:12, 17, 19-20)

What Paul is saying is that an afterlife that will essentially cancel out all the problems of this life is coming for the faithful. However, in our this-worldly interpretation of Jesus and of Christian faith, there is no basis for such a claim: the conception of an afterlife presupposes the notion of an "other world" to which faithful believers go after death. Though this notion has been held by many through much of Christian history, it has not been accepted by all Christians in the past (according to Paul's letter, just quoted, this disbelief goes back to the early days of the church); and there are many Christians today for whom both the traditional dualistic two-worlds notion and the anthropomorphic conception of God that accompanies it are simply unbelievable. The rejection of these traditional claims is, of course, central to the theology with which we are working here. And this implies that traditional Christian eschatology must also go. We humans are simply not in a position to *know* what the ultimate future of our universe will be; or the ultimate future of our human world within this universe; or about some life-after-death to which some or all humans will ultimately go. We can, however, say this about the future: it certainly may be *hoped* that the creativity (God) that brought us into being, and which still sustains and enhances the order of life on planet Earth, will continue—for a considerable future—the sustenance and enhancement of the biohistorical trajectory on which we humans find ourselves.

When we look back over the past in our corner of the universe, observing the creativity manifest everywhere in it, we see the complex of creative trajectories that brought life into being on planet Earth—and, as part of that life, brought human existence into being; and we are drawn to acknowledge the great gifts that creativity—God!—has bestowed upon us humans, especially the gift of active participation in the creation of the human trajectory itself. Love, forgiveness, hope, joy, peace, justice, courage, humility, moral responsibility—above all, our own human creativity—all came into being as this trajectory moved forward, creating and sustaining important cultural and religious values and meanings, dispositions and practices and institutions. In the course of these developments a context emerged within which Jesus appeared, and not long after that the image/story of Jesus-trajectory$_1$ was created. Although the two-worlds picture that informed that story may no longer be plausible to us, Jesus-trajectory$_2$ supplies us with a version of the Jesus-story that is completely this-worldly. This picture can inform the desires and intentions of the many today who wish to commit (or re-commit) themselves to the powerful stream of creativity (God) that has been manifest in and through Jesus and the Jesus-movement during the last two millennia. As we all proceed into the future, we can hope this movement will gain the insight and the strength to bring new forms of "abundant life" (John 10:10) into our seriously fractured world. What this future will actually bring is, of course, unknown to us; nevertheless, Christians can commit themselves to the hope that the stream of ongoing creativity that Jesus-trajectory$_2$ reveals to us—that mysterious creativity (God) that has brought this trajectory into being—will continue to provide a context within which we can effectively address the important problems we today face. In chapter 4 I will say something about the particular problems I have in mind here, and about the respects in which the image/story of Jesus may be of importance in addressing them.

In all of this we have been reflecting on the connection of God (creativity) with the Jesus-story and the continuing effects of that ongoing creativity. The actual historicity in Jesus' life of some aspects of that story is not as important an issue as the *creative effects* of that life and death. In my view this way of thinking about the Jesus-event—in terms of its creativity—dissolves away the Jesus-of-history versus Christ-of-faith debate almost completely. And it allows for, and in fact plays up in a significant way, an ongoing creative spirit, a spirit that the images and stories of Jesus and the early Christians continue to inspire. Like all humans, we today live out of our historicity and what it has bequeathed to us, and we live anticipating a largely unknown future. But it is in the *present*, not the past or the future, that our ongoing living, thinking, deciding, and acting occur.

V

Although many today regard Jesus-trajectory$_1$ as too implausible to take seriously, they may find that one of the versions of the image/story of Jesus in trajectory$_2$ draws them powerfully to itself and can create in their lives meaning, order, and orientation in today's pluralistic world. And they may gratefully acknowledge that God—the mystery of creativity, the ultimate source of our existence in the world—continues today to be profoundly involved with us humans in our living and our dying. This observation might well lead to questions about the implications that the understanding of God and of Jesus with which we are working in this book might have for such religious practices as prayer and worship. In the past much Christian worship and prayer has presupposed an anthropomorphic and anthropocentric God, a God who "hears our prayers" and who "answers" them; and Jesus has traditionally been understood as a resurrected personal being "sitting at the right hand of God the Father" and ruling the world as its "Lord" and "Savior." Given that context, it is not surprising that prayer—whether directed to Jesus or to God—was often thought of on the model of *conversation*, a conversation between living personal beings. And worship was thought of as bowing down before, or looking up reverently toward, the creator of the universe. These practices, however, are obviously no longer appropriate for those who take seriously the conceptions of God and of Jesus with which we have been working here.

This does not imply that there is no longer any place in our lives for worship and prayer. The God with which we are concerned here is the wondrous *serendipitous creativity* that has brought us humans into being within this magnificent universe—this universe that continues to be creatively transformed in new and surprising ways. It is a universe of great beauty and of overwhelming displays of power; a universe populated by many utterly diverse kinds of beings; a universe within which, on planet Earth (and possibly elsewhere) living beings in countless varieties have been created—including our own human mode of existence. This is a universe and a creativity that call forth profound feelings of awe, appreciation, and gratitude—that is, basic modes of worship and prayer. And as we contemplate the profound *mystery* of this creativity and the vast complex universe it has brought forth, we are moved to *meditate* on it at length—another mode of both public and private prayer and worship. And we may find ourselves uttering prayers and singing songs of praise and thanksgiving to this wondrous God, this serendipitous creativity, and uttering prayers of contrition and penitence for marring this beautiful world by our faults and failures, our self-centeredness and greed, our sins against our fellow-humans, against the living environment in which we find ourselves, and against the creativity that has brought us forth in this magnificent world—two more modes of prayer and worship. It is important for us humans to express our joys and our gratitude, our sorrows and our pains, our fears and our hopes, our problems and our achievements in whatever words—or whatever silent meditation—seem to us a right and proper way to acknowledge all these matters. This may lead us to one more mode of worship and prayer: our profound privilege to give ourselves over to this deep mystery of creativity—this creativity that has also, through the mission and ministry of Jesus of Nazareth in life, in death, and after his death, brought into our world the practice of *agape*-love and shown us its profound meaningfulness and value. This deep mystery of creativity thus becomes a *light* enabling us to see more clearly how we ought to live and act as we move forward into the unknown future.

chapter three

Humans as Biohistorical Beings: Historicity, Creativity, Freedom

In chapters 1 and 2 of this book we have explored some of the implications for *christology* of my suggestion that we understand God as *creativity*, creativity as *God*. The symbol of *God* and the symbol of *Jesus* are both, of course, human imaginative constructs. They were created as men and women—through drawing on traditions going back especially to ancient Israel, on the one hand, and Greece and Rome, on the other—sought to orient themselves and order their lives in face of the many problems they needed to address in the worlds in which they found themselves. Why have humans—as they sought to work their way through the problems and difficulties of ordinary daily life—created such elaborate, widely comprehensive symbols as these? What is there about human existence that leads men and women into such speculative activities? To understand these matters adequately, and thus to be in a position to assess the continuing importance of these two central Christian symbols, we need to examine certain distinctive features of our humanness. In chapter 2 I suggested that it is useful to think of humans as *biohistorical* beings. We are a unique species with capabilities of acting, thinking, and creating unmatched by any other form of life; and it is because of these capabilities—and the problems that arise in connection with them—that symbols such as *Jesus* and *God* have

63

been created (over many generations) and continue to be cherished. They provide a way of orienting and ordering human life at the most fundamental and comprehensive levels. In this chapter we will explore these necessities and thereby put ourselves in a position to examine more fully, in chapter 4, the significance of the symbol Jesus—in its interconnectedness with the symbol God—that we have been working out in this book.

I

The word "biohistorical" holds together in one both the biological grounding of our human existence and the historico-cultural dimensions of human life, thus highlighting what is most distinctive in our humanness.[1] It immediately suggests that we are qualitatively different from any other form of life in important respects. We humans emerged—out of less complex or (as some would say) "lower" forms of life—in the course of evolutionary developments on planet Earth over many millennia; and we cannot exist apart from this living web that continues to nourish and sustain us. It is important to note that this biological point by itself tells us nothing about the unique role, within this evolutionary setting, played by the emerging *historical* features (that is, the sociocultural features) of human existence. The order of nature is, of course, the wider context within which human history has appeared, but it has been especially through our historical sociocultural development over many millennia—not our biological evolution alone—that we humans have acquired many of our most distinctive characteristics. Our increasingly comprehensive knowledge, for example, about the natural world in which we live and about our human constitution and possibilities has provided us with significant powers over our immediate environment and over the physical and biological, as well as sociocultural and psychological, conditions of our existence—powers that go far beyond those of any other animal. We humans, thus, have gained, in and through our various knowledges, a measure of transcendence over the nature of which we are part; and with our developing practices and skills—growing in modernity into enormously powerful technologies—we have utterly transformed the face of the earth and are beginning to push on into outer space. Clearly we human beings, and the further course of human history, are no longer completely at the disposal of the natural order and natural powers that brought us into being, in the way we were, say, ten millennia ago.

How should we understand—in connection with the evolutionary account—these features of our humanity that have emerged largely in human history? Anthropologist Clifford Geertz has pointed out that our present biological organisms, if left simply to themselves, would be so seriously deficient that they could not function. "We are ... incomplete or unfinished animals who complete or finish ourselves through culture—and not through culture in general but through highly particular forms of it: Dobuan and Javanese, Hopi and Italian, upper-class, academic and commercial" (Geertz 1973:49). The organism that has finally appeared as human is, thus, "both a cultural and a biological product";[2] and the various sorts of human culture that have appeared around the world must each be understood as an indispensable dimension—in its particular location—of the *niche* on planet Earth within which humankind is sustained. Our niche, without which we humans could never have come into being or continued in being, has increasingly acquired important historico-cultural features: that is, the human niche is itself a developing biohistorical reality. This cultural dimension of human existence, including especially the growth and increasing complexity of human symbolic behaviors, has affected significantly the actual *biological* development of the predecessors of today's *Homo sapiens*. It has had particularly strong effects on the evolution of the human brain, as brain-scientist Terrence Deacon has shown. Deacon argues that the emergence of symbolic behaviors—such as language, a central feature in the historical unfolding of human cultural life—helped bring about the evolution of our unusually large brains (Deacon 1997:44–46, 251f., 339–59, 407–10). Thus, all the way down to the deepest roots of our distinctly *human* existence, we are not simply biological beings, animals; we are *biohistorical* beings. And in significant respects, our growing historicalness—our *historicity*—is the most distinctive mark of our humanness.

Because of our historicity—because we are beings shaped decisively by histories that have in turn given us the power to shape future history in significant ways—we humans have great creative and destructive powers in the natural order on planet Earth. And in the last century, we have become aware that unless we live and act within the constraints that life's ecological order on Earth places on us—unless we arrange our activities in ways appropriate to the environmental context that supports and sustains us—we will not survive much longer. No other form of life—trees, dogs, other primates—needs this kind of information or would be able to make any use of it. We humans alone have knowledges and technologies that give us the power to destroy ourselves as well as many other complex forms of life; and, in fact, we are already engaged in such highly destructive activity. We humans alone are able to envision the enormity of these matters—to understand what all of this means (not only for ourselves but for other species as well); and we alone are able deliberately to amend our ways in respects that may bring us into better harmony with the overall ecology of planet Earth. For us humans, thus, these concerns have become a matter of life and death—not only for ourselves but for much other life as well. Humans are *historical* beings—beings with *historicity*, agents with powers to shape their own future: if we are to survive in this world, not to mention flourish, we need to develop an understanding of ourselves and the world in which we live that makes clear how we must comport ourselves in life, how we must live and act; our understanding of ourselves, that is, must include moral and ethical features.

In every age and every society and culture about which we have some knowledge, we find what we today call "religious" and "moral" dimensions. Women and men everywhere have created (have imagined) pictures and conceptions of the world in which they were living— conceptions of what human beings are; of rules and standards, values and norms, governing how life should be lived; and of institutions assuring that these important matters would be passed on to future generations. In acquiring language and culture every normal infant begins to order its behavior in terms of what, in due course, will become exceedingly detailed and complex socially created and socially imposed rules and norms—behavioral patterns within which it will live and act and think throughout the rest of its life. Language, many other behavioral practices and normative standards, and world-pictures—not this or that specific linguistic or moral rule, or cultural value, or conception of the context of human life, but the necessity to have such values and rules and conceptions—belong to our humanity as such, to our self-consciousness and our capacity to take responsibility for ourselves in some measure. These are central features of the historical dimensions of our human existence. I want now to sketch briefly some of the characteristics of this normativity that is apparently inherent in our humanness. I shall make five points in this connection.[3]

Anthropological constants [handwritten marginal note]

1. That which most sharply differentiates human beings from other forms of life (as we have just been noting) is our historicity: on the one hand, we humans have been shaped by our histories; but on the other hand, increasingly we have—especially during recent millennia—gained significant control over some of the processes of historical change and development through which we are moving, and in that respect some degree of control over our own historicity. Our growing human powers and creativity, however, have obviously become quite dangerous, and we must strive to manage them better or we may destroy ourselves. We need, therefore, to think through carefully how we humans—as a species—should proceed at this point.

2. Human beings; human institutions, cultures, and societies; and human historical processes—all of these marked by historicity—could not have come into existence or remained in existence without delicate balances between creativity and continuity, freedom and order, in the cultures within which they were emerging. The maintenance of such balances in communal institutions and practices, and in individual agents and their actions, is what can be called "responsible" ordering and acting. An optimal realization of human historicity in any particular concrete situation can occur only to the extent that the pertinent communities and selves are able and willing to take significant *responsibility* for their institutions, practices, and actions; this responsibility, of course, is understood in quite different ways in the many diverse sociocultural and historical contexts in which it emerges. (The concepts of "responsible" and "responsibility" will be examined in some detail later in this chapter. Here I use these words in their conventional meanings.)

3. As we look back over the history of the past century—with its horrible paroxysms of violence and war, but also its enormous growth in human knowledges and powers—we can see how important it is that we exercise our historicity in much more responsible ordering and action than we have achieved in the past. We must shape and reshape our human communities and selves in ways that—as we hope—will

facilitate the development of better-ordered freedom and creativity in both the individuals and the societies of future humankind. The enormous growth of our technological power in recent centuries, culminating in the power to destroy humanity along with many other species of life, means that only as we humans learn to take greater responsibility for the effects of our actions—on both the environment and the ongoing movement and direction of history and culture—can there be much likelihood that we will survive.

4. Our capacity to take responsibility for ourselves and for the direction history is going depends on a relatively high degree of self-consciousness and knowledge of what we are actually doing and its effects, and a proper orienting of that consciousness and knowledge in action. The effectiveness of our historicity will depend significantly on our awareness of ourselves and our powers and of what our real possibilities in life may be, as well as on the existence of practices and institutions that facilitate the historical dimensions of our lives. If humanity is to survive and flourish, we will have to work toward patterns of societal organization, practices, and institutions that will expand and deepen awareness of our historicity and its significance; these must include social and cultural patterns that will sustain and perhaps enhance our historicity. Obviously, the many forms these issues and concerns take in various sociocultural contexts and for different persons cannot be specified in this bare outline: those matters will depend on the specific, very diverse situations involved.

5. In all these matters, of course, we must keep in mind that our historicity cannot function optimally unless it is working harmoniously with its biological base—our bodies and the ecological networks that sustain and support them—and only if that biological base is itself functioning well. Taking responsibility for ourselves and our societies as biohistorical beings must always include, therefore, taking significant responsibility for the organic and physical networks of which we are part.

These normative considerations, grounded in and emergent from the historicity of our humanness, are quite abstract and formal as here sketched; and in that respect they violate the very concern for historicity that I am trying to express. To hold, for example (in point 1, above), that the overarching consideration that we must take into account is the imperative "to think through carefully how we humans—as a species—should proceed at this point" leaves this central concern in much too abstract a form. The whole point of calling attention to our "historicity" is to emphasize that our understanding of what is required of us in any particular situation is always shaped largely by the historico-natural situation itself, not by some abstract universal norm. What is required by one sociohistorical situation or natural setting will likely be significantly different from what is required in other contexts. In this book, for example, we are concerned with the question of what significance Jesus may have in today's world. But obviously there cannot be any single answer to such a vague and general question as that. What that question may signify for Chinese peasants would likely be of little interest to modern European university students, and vice versa; what may be important in that question for some African politicians would hardly be of pertinence to American soldiers in Iraq or Afghanistan, and vice versa. The conception of us humans as fundamentally historical beings has itself developed in a particular historical context—largely among intellectuals in the modern West. Like all other conceptions, it has its meaning, significance, and truth principally within that context, and the extent to which it will be taken seriously into account in other situations will depend very much on those situations themselves. It should not be surprising, therefore, if some of the abstract concepts found in this discussion may at first make little sense to some readers. It is my hope that reading this chapter will clarify these matters.

The fourth point above, that taking "responsibility for ourselves and for the direction history is going" presupposes knowledge that we are historical beings, and this requires a "relatively high degree of self-consciousness," is also extremely abstract and thus potentially misleading. The level of our self-consciousness, as well as the kind of self-consciousness that we have, depends largely on the particular historico-cultural situation within which we live and think. It is not the case that everyone in the world at this moment can understand, or needs to understand, himself or herself as a "historical being"; modes and degrees of consciousness of this fact differ greatly in the countless varied local situations around the world—a point directly implied in the claim that we are shaped by and relative to our basic historical contexts.

This consideration, moreover, will be pertinent rather differently for those with the power to affect and take responsibility for large populations than for those, for instance, with a newly emerging consciousness of their own oppression—a point often emphasized by liberation theologians. Observations similar to these could easily be made about the other points being considered here.

As historical, self-conscious, culture-creating, and in some respects self-determining beings, women and men inevitably must decide what they are to do and be—given the life-situations in which they find themselves: How should they shape and order and orient their lives? Toward what sort of future should they work? It is not the case, of course, that all men and women have thought of themselves as free and creative, as able to shape and determine their own futures and their children's futures. In some cultures ideas of this sort have not appeared, or have been downplayed; and in most cultures they have been deemphasized for women. Thus, the forms in which experience has come to many individuals and groups have often inhibited these notes from coming into view. However, the modern intellectual standpoints that enable us to observe the great variety of cultures, societies, and religions—all of which have been produced by the human spirit—put us into a position from which we can hardly avoid thinking of that spirit as possessing great freedom and creative power. It is important that both societies and individuals learn to take significant responsibility for themselves and their worlds: what men and women decide today, especially and most frighteningly in the realms of international politics, economics, and ecological concerns, will significantly affect the life of future generations—indeed, it may determine whether there will be many more generations in the future.

Our international political arrangements have put the gradually cumulating growth of human power during our long history into the hands of nations competing with each other (though economic developments in the last century have somewhat qualified this point); and our moral and religious commitments and values and suspicions—especially in the fundamentalistic versions now appearing many places around the globe—focus the energies and interests of each of us on the political, economic, cultural, and religious *fragment* of humanity to which we belong, rather than on the well-being of humanity as a whole and the welfare of the rest of life on Earth. So our moralities and our religions and our other value-loyalties, instead of enlarging and protect-ing our well-being, actually increase the possibilities of disastrous wars.[4] Instead of acceding to the demands of our present social, political, and religious commitments and arrangements, we men and women today must take up our full responsibilities and act in behalf of humanity as a whole—and in behalf of our environment, which makes all life on Earth possible.

II

Humans are socioculturally shaped and socioculturally creative beings, as we have been noting; and as a result of our creativity we have gradu-ally acquired the power to shape significantly—that is, to participate in the *creation* of—our human future. As far as we know, creativity of this self-conscious sort is found only in the human world, and it did not come about in any simple way. Human deliberative creativity could hardly have begun before the development of fully articulate speech, possibly one hundred thousand to two hundred thousand years ago (Deacon 1997:364). Let us imagine, for a moment, how our creativity may have come into being (been created). The initial stages must have been largely social developments, possibly brought about by the growing *intensity* of the more or less primitive linguistic interchanges, a seren-dipitous outcome of the wider creativity in the universe (God); these beginnings certainly could not have been the result of any deliberate human intentions and actions (for no one could have had any idea of creativity at that point). However, as humans increasingly gained facility with language, they discovered a deeper solidarity with each other, new possibilities of collective action and enjoyment, and new kinds of experi-ence. The more they interacted linguistically, the more complex became their interconnectedness. This in turn encouraged still more linguistic interaction, which led to increasingly intricate linguistic patterns, and so on: language as an enormously complex symbolic system was beginning to come on the scene. So what began simply as ordinary natural inter-actions between different members of the species *Homo sapiens* evolved serendipitously (over many generations) into modes of sociocultural interaction that were more complex and experientially rewarding, and thus preferred over other modes. In this way the possibility of choice—

deliberate decision—was beginning to appear (be created), and with it came the possibility of *creating* this rather than that. In all of this the human brain was itself being constrained to grow and develop.

It is worth noting that the serendipitous creativity (God) to which I have been calling attention here is similarly involved in the development of every new human infant: over many months an infant gradually pulls together and organizes the vast swarm of feelings and images and noises; muscular throbbing and bodily struggling; the regularity of appearances and actions of caretakers together with the special comfort and relief felt when fed, when diapers have been changed, when being warmly held and gently rocked and otherwise responded to; and so on and so on. As the infant gradually brings all this "blooming buzzing confusion" (William James) into increasingly familiar patterns—largely shaped by the language it is beginning to acquire—a sense of its own self and a sense of being in relatively organized surroundings slowly develop. None of the earliest steps into this emerging linguistic facility, growing self-consciousness, and incipient ability to make choices can be directly intended or chosen by the infant, for each of these capacities is only in the process of being created—*serendipitously* created—in connection with the infant's continuous interaction with its caregivers. Similarly with the historical emergence of our species into self-consciousness and the abilities to speak and act: the early stages were largely a serendipitous product of complex processes of interaction over many generations. Along with the gradual emergence of language, self-consciousness, and deliberate choice—in the early history of the human race, as well as in the development of each human infant—a wide range of skills and capacities began to emerge and come into play. In both cases creative processes that originally begin serendipitously (God) gradually become a complex intermix of this serendipitous creativity with some degree of deliberate human choice and action.

This mix of human self-conscious creativity with the serendipitous creativity roundabout has continued all the way down to the present, with the proportion of deliberate human creative action steadily growing. As the creation of increasingly complex languages and cultures continued, and human self-consciousness emerged more fully and began to direct human activities more effectively, women and men gradually learned how to make plans and develop long-term projects. Thus, the creation—in part humanly intended, in part serendipitous (God)—of increasingly intricate cultures continued to move onward; and in connection with that movement, more complex modes of action as well as new ways of thinking emerged. We still experience, in the projects with which we humans are engaged today, this intricate mix of deliberate human intention and action with the serendipitous contextual creativity that brings about quite unexpected developments—some desirable (from a human point of view) and some exceedingly undesirable. This occurrence of "unexpected consequences" of our human actions is often remarked upon.[5] Another well-known example of this contextual creativity is sometimes experienced in ordinary conversation:

> A conversation . . . is not simply an interchange of discrete "acts," in which each agent is attempting to realize a particular goal. Though in each remark the speaker is attempting to say something that is fitting at that moment, what happens in a conversation cannot be understood simply as the summing up of all these individual actions. Often the interchange comes to have "a life of its own" (as we say), and it may well go in directions no one had anticipated and lead to new insights and ideas which none of the participants had thought of before. . . . Thus . . . the conversation proceeds down pathways not expected by the original speaker or any of the others. An intervention by speaker B moves the conversation in a way that A had not intended; and a succeeding intervention by C moves down a slightly different path, not anticipated by either A or B, so that when A responds again, it will be with a comment not directly continuous with his or her earlier remark, one which takes into account what B and C have unexpectedly said. And thus the path of the conversation as a whole, though definitely continuous, is not a direct working out of the original intention which A (or anyone else) was attempting to express. . . . Sometimes, in an exciting conversation of this sort where new ideas seem continuously to be bursting forth, the participants are "carried away" by the flow of the conversation itself, which has come to have a seeming intention of its own. . . . This social experience . . . does not mean that the individuals cease to act as free agents in their own right: they each contribute

to the conversation out of their own freedom, not under some external compulsion . . . ; it is a moment of [serendipitous] creativity which the group process itself makes possible. (Kaufman 1993:275f.)

Our human ability to act, I am suggesting, is bound up closely with our creativity—as well as with the wider serendipitous creativity (God) that seemingly appears almost everywhere. Conversely, our human creativity is bound up closely with our ability to *act*—our ability to make decisions about what we want to do, to plan the course of action that will enable us to accomplish what we have decided upon, and then to work on that program until our intentions have been realized (or changed). All human actions and procedures can quite properly be regarded as instances of creativity—a low grade of creativity, perhaps, but creativity nonetheless—for they are intended to bring into being something that did not exist before, something new.

These sorts of daily activities are all quite familiar and frequent and are usually not thought of as particularly important or creative. We generally reserve the words "creative" and "creativity" for quite unusual events in which something extraordinary, very important, and previously non-existent has been brought into being; the thought of *creating something truly new* has a ring of special significance, rarity, novelty. I have no desire to change this note of special significance that is suggested when the notion of creativity is invoked.[6] But it is important—especially as we consider our human *historicity* in connection with the theological position being developed here—that we understand the close link of human creativity with ordinary human agency and that we do not assume that only geniuses or gods can engage in this supposedly miraculous activity. None of these three—human historicity, agency, creativity—can be conceived apart from the others; these features of our humanness must have gradually evolved and developed, over many millennia, in interconnection with each other.[7]

Though our creativity could not exist apart from our historicity and agency, in some respects it may be regarded as the most important of the three. Without this creativity—in part the emerging creativity of humans themselves, in part the surrounding serendipitous creativity (God)—humans would never have been able to transform the context of their activities and lives from the strictly natural order within which they originally emerged into a gradually evolving system of dynamic transgenerational *biohistorical* momentums. This new, slowly emerging biohistorical order began to provide a context within which (at least in some settings) further human creativity would be encouraged and could become effective. As humans faced the problems that arose in their ordinary everyday living, human creativity was occurring with increasing potency and frequency. Obviously we cannot take up here the many examples of creativity in everyday life, but we need to note that none of this human creativity would have emerged had human life not been gradually acquiring a bio*historical* form: humans were animals that, for many thousands of years, lived out their lives in the context of increasingly complex *sociocultural* worlds. These sociocultural worlds—slowly and quite unintentionally created by our many generations of forebears as they addressed the problems they had to face—provide the basic settings of our lives today, contexts handed down to each of us as we were socialized and enculturated from infancy.

We have been examining here the structural features that had to emerge if human agency was going to appear and develop. An agent is a *self-conscious* subject,[8] an "I," a being not only aware of the various features and dimensions of the world in which it is acting but also implicitly aware of itself and its feelings, desires, wishes, moods, attitudes, abilities and skills, hopes and dreams, loves and hates, successes and failures. Of course, some persons, perhaps because of unusual circumstances of class or role or education, may be much more conscious of their agency than others. Agency and responsibility—and our sense of agency and responsibility—vary greatly in strength and significance from moment to moment, person to person, group to group, culture to culture; and no individual person or social group, no culture or class or gender or race or historical period, is entirely devoid of all possibilities for responsible action (barring, of course, a major disastrous breakdown).

Our brief examination here of the complex interconnectedness of human historicity, agency, and creativity—each of them dependent upon the emerging human linguistic capabilities—should give us some sense of the complicated and lengthy biohistorical development apart from which this triad central to our humanness could not have emerged (been created). As we have noted, this development is reenacted in its own distinctive way as each new human being moves from birth through infancy, childhood, and adolescence into full maturity.

III

With this developmental picture of our humanness in mind, we are in a position to turn to the question of *responsible* agency and creativity; and that will bring us closer to an understanding of what such comprehensive symbols as God and Jesus are all about. We rarely, if ever, talk about animals (or computers!) "taking responsibility" for a given situation or action, though we are well aware that animals are able to "care for" their young, can be taught to behave in ways required by humans (as a result of housebreaking of pets, for example), and can learn to "obey" many different sorts of human commands. Though we may say that we hold our dog "responsible" for having made a mess in the kitchen, it would seem a little odd to say the dog ought to "take responsibility" for this sort of problem. *Taking responsibility* is an extraordinarily complicated sort of action that perhaps only the human brain can manage. One must have acquired a number of complex skills and abilities (with their respective feedback mechanisms) and have learned how to manage all of these in concert when contemplating a future course of action for which one is willing to hold oneself *responsible*.[9] Many animals have the capacity to seek necessary or desirable goals (for example, to search for food, engage in mating, make nests, travel great distances without getting lost), and that suggests their possession of something like rudimentary forms of what in humans develop into self-conscious attention and intention. But to "take responsibility" for what we are doing or are attempting to do, we need a good deal more than the capacity to seek desirable goals.

We must, for example, be able to *imagine* the future—that is, imagine what is not now the case and thus not present in our experience. Indeed, we must be able to imagine more or less simultaneously a number of diverse possible futures among which we might choose as we contemplate alternative actions that could be undertaken. For such imagining to be possible, we must have acquired a complex but manageable symbol/image system in terms of which we can represent to ourselves these diverse alternatives. This is ordinarily made available to humans as we acquire a complex language in the early years of life, a language that, above all, has first-person words such as "I," "me," "mine," "we," "us." First-person terms all have *self-reflexiveness* built into them. In saying "I" or "me" a speaker is paying attention and calling attention to himself or herself (along with whatever else it is that he or she is saying). In learning to say "I" (at about the age of two years) we were beginning to distinguish ourselves clearly from things other than ourselves—from all those things with which the "I" enables us to contrast ourselves. Thus, we began to bring about (create) what is called "*self*-consciousness." (Similarly with "we" and "us" and "our"—words which enable us to be aware of ourselves as participating members of specific groups.)[10] The language that we learn in early childhood, together with the facility that this enormously complex symbol-system provides us, makes possible our acquisition of a number of important skills and capacities: our ability to symbolize, intend, attend, decide, and so on; our self-awareness and self-consciousness; an enormous extension of our capacity to imagine; and much else. Without these instrumentalities, human *agency* (acting *deliberately*) and human *taking responsibility* for our actions, our selves, and our human creativity would not be possible.

When we hold ourselves responsible for something we have done, or understand that we must take responsibility for what we are about to do, we are making reflexive moves in our minds that go an important step further than first-person language alone could carry us. To take responsibility is to make a move that binds agent/decision/intention/attention/act/creativity all together in a larger unity, a newly created unity in which the act and creativity performed are directly attributed to the agent. The agent is now regarded, and regards herself or himself, as the dynamic origin or source of the act, as well as of the creativity that comes about through the act. Neither of these would have occurred without this agency, and for this reason the agent is held accountable for both of them. Here the peculiar character of human self-consciousness—that it relates itself to itself, that it is self-reflexive in unique and important ways—again appears, but in a more complex mode than simply saying "I." And the act is itself a novel *creation*, a creation that brings about the further creation of something that did not exist before.

We are now in a better position to see how and why being *responsible*, taking *responsibility* for our selves and our actions, is so important.

Complex forms of human existence are constituted by biohistorical structures and processes of the sort just mentioned, and the complexity of these forms could neither come into being nor continue without them. The triad of human historicity/action/creativity is a fragile *living* structure. I say "living" because, as a biohistorical process, its continuing existence depends on the ongoing activities of living human beings. If and when all humans engaged in a specific instance of this process die, the process itself—and the many diverse living strands of which it is constituted—will die with them. They may leave behind wonderful artifacts—think of Easter Island, for instance[11]—but many of those artifacts will no longer have use or meaning. Unless we humans in all our diverse cultural settings—Africans and Chinese, Indonesians and Americans, farmers and CEOs, teachers and politicians, mothers and fathers, and so on—continue to take responsibility for the particular strands of our common biohistorical heritages, those strands will die away (though some of their features may survive in other cultures they have influenced). Recently we humans have learned that in our ongoing activities—creative and destructive—we are undermining the very conditions that make human biohistorical life, and much other life as well, possible. The time has thus come for us humans *as a whole* to take responsibility for the human project as a whole; that is, to take more direct responsibility than we have in the past for the ongoing living triad of human historicity/action/creativity. If we do not, the human project itself may not survive much longer. In chapter 4 we will consider whether and in what respects the central Christian symbols with which we are working, "Jesus" and "God" (creativity), bear significantly on this urgent matter.

To take responsibility for some act or project or person or community is, in the first place, to *respond* to it, to become concerned about it; and in the second place, to make ourselves *accountable* for it—to keep ourselves informed about its well-being, and if there are problems to seek ways to address them effectively.[12] Something like taking responsibility is to be found in all human cultures. All activities directed toward keeping the complex living interactive networks of human affairs properly oiled and working, so that the day-by-day exigencies of life can be effectively addressed, come under this heading. A good physician is someone who takes responsibility for patients who need special care because of illness or accident. A good teacher is one who takes responsibility to educate students—that is, to introduce them to various features of the culture in which they are growing up and within which they expect to live so they come to enjoy and to participate effectively, happily, and creatively in those aspects of their ongoing lives. Good parents are those who take responsibility for their children so that they remain healthy, become enabled to fit well in the sociocultural context in which they will likely be living, get a good education, and—above all—are able to grow into, and will seek to become, responsible adults. Many of our specifically *moral* terms ("trustworthy," "good," "loyal," "liar," "honest," "cheat," "courageous," and so on) direct our attention to various distinct features of responsible (and irresponsible) acting and living (Kaufman 1993:189–91); and we ordinarily employ these and other similar terms when we want to encourage ourselves and others to act responsibly in particular situations. The words "responsible" and "responsibility" (and, of course, "irresponsible") are important flags with which we call attention to potential major breakdowns of the complex historicity/action/creativity triad, breakdowns that threaten the human biohistorical project.

Taking responsibility is a capacity of a higher, more complex order than the skills and activities earlier mentioned (that is, speaking, imagining, symbolizing, deciding, intending, attending), and it presupposes them all.[13] To be an agent, as we can now see, is not merely to be one who can do something: it is to be one who is held accountable for what he or she does and who holds herself or himself accountable. The agent knows that it is not enough to think of oneself as simply choosing between envisaged alternatives; one must also recognize that one is *accountable* for the choice that is made and accountable for the way in which the act is carried out. This accountability is in due course factored back into the process of decision-making; and choices then begin to be made, intentions advanced, and actions performed with the issue of accountability also considered. Accountability thus constitutes another feedback loop in the self-reflexiveness of the agent, and this sense of responsibility or accountability becomes a feature of the self-awareness of the agent as further acts are envisaged. So a new and more complex level of symbolization and self-consciousness begins to pervade the whole process of acting, a level that deepens significantly the sense of one's agency and all that is involved in one's decisions and actions. What is emerging (being created) here is *moral* agency. With it comes the necessity to find ways of assessing the sorts of acts for which one is willing to be held accountable, distinguishing them from those for which one does not wish to take responsibility. And this gives rise to an entirely new consideration: the question about standards and norms that define responsible conduct and can thus provide guidance in our deciding and acting—what we call *moral* standards and values, moral rules and norms. The possibility—and the necessity—of making distinctions between moral and immoral, good and bad, right and wrong action has thus emerged (been created).

The emergence of moral standards and rules—of some form of moral language and with it *morality*—is no accident: it has been essential for survival in every society. Without some distinctions of this sort, and without their importance being emphasized by penalties for violations, the complex networks that make increasingly complicated action and creativity possible would probably never have developed or been sustained. These sorts of activity become possible and effective only when, on the one hand, there are in the society quite complex social networks of differentiated roles and statuses, clear behavioral patterns, well-developed linguistic and ideological traditions, and the like. In individuals, on the other hand, there must be complex feedback networks of body control, significant behavioral patterns and skills, good linguistic facility, mental training, and discipline.[14] Every new act performed will have its effect upon and will make its contribution to this complex interconnected web that is indispensable for ongoing deliberate action and creativity. Agents—whether individuals or communities—are, of course, just as responsible for these wider consequences of their acts as for their more immediate objectives. It has been through the growth of complicated networks over many generations that these sorts of complex action have become possible, and it is only through the *responsible* exercise of human agency that they can be sustained and further developed. When we ask the distinctively *moral* questions—Is it *right* to do that? Is it *good* to do that? Is it *wrong* or *evil* to do that?—we are asking whether this particular act is a piece of *responsible doing*. That is, we are asking whether this act fits effectively and appropriately into the surrounding action-network into which it is being introduced, asking thus about its *quality* as a responsible *act*—in the full, rich sense of the word "act."

This is something significantly different from asking whether the act is, say, "expedient" or whether it "fits" well within its immediate context.[15] In our *moral* questioning we ask about such things as these: Is the intention expressed in the act a responsible one? That is, does it take into account all that should be taken into account in connection with this act? Has the act been carried through in a responsible way? Is the agent (whether a person, a community, a church, a corporation, a nation) acting responsibly in performing this act? However important may be concerns about expediency or aesthetic matters, questions like these that involve *moral* reflection and criticism raise the most funda-mental and far-reaching issues, for here we are inquiring about and assessing action in its distinctive character as free and responsible doing by selves and communities. Every action is a new link in the complex sociocultural web apart from which no acts would be possible: will this act strengthen that web or weaken it? Of course, in many of the trivial decisions we make, these wider effects and more general characteristics of our actions remain largely unnoticed and are relatively unimportant. But with our weightier choices we feel impelled to take into account this more far-reaching significance of what we are about to do. This question about the ramifications of our actions on the action-networks in both our society and ourselves is the deep root of what we call *morality*.

One more consideration bearing on human responsibility must be mentioned here. We cannot act responsibly unless we have awareness of, and fairly accurate knowledge about, the *context* within which we are about to act: Are there bears in the woods into which we propose to go? poisonous plants to be avoided? possible resources of food and shelter if needed? safe places to spend the night? and so on. It is of course pos-sible, and sometimes necessary, to move into a situation about which one knows very little, but such moves may be quite dangerous and foolhardy. So when risky moves are about to be undertaken, an agent—whether group or individual—concerned about acting responsibly will attempt to acquire as much valid information as possible. We could not act at all if we had no awareness of at least the basic outlines of the situation into which we were moving; without that we would have no way of deciding what to do, what act would be appropriate.

In every society, of course, an important part of the enculturation with which children are provided is awareness and knowledge of the surroundings in which they are living. Such knowledge is ordinarily not taught in explicit verbal lessons in which we would say, for example, "This is walking, and that is sitting, and this is a chair, and that is a table, and this is how we walk to the chair and sit at the table." Rather, the child is simply helped to engage in the activities of walking and sitting and eating at the table; and the pertinent language is picked up as he or she acquires these important skills and practices. The child gradually becomes aware of being in the house, and aware of the yard outside the house, and aware of the dangers on the street. Quite unconsciously the child builds up (creates) a picture of his or her immediate environment; and in the subsequent years of growth the picture becomes augmented by the child's accumulating experience, on the one hand, and augmented very substantially, on the other hand, by the child's growing awareness of the larger picture of the wider surrounding world. By adolescence and later maturity the child will have acquired major features of the *world-picture* dominant in the society within which he or she is growing up.[16] That is, the child will have become aware of the many features of the basic context within which his or her activities are carried out—a world-picture that will be largely taken for granted in all future acting, thinking, planning, exploring, meditating, and ongoing living. Most children will live out their lives, of course, in the context supplied by the dominant world-picture(s) of the culture(s) in which they have been socialized; and women and men, who in their maturity seek to act responsibly, ordinarily envision, understand, and work out their actions in the terms supplied by these cultural world-pictures that, in their local and cosmic dimensions, order and orient their lives. Without these "pictures" of the wider contexts in which we take ourselves to be living—pictures of which we may barely be consciously aware—there could not be any responsible action; and without responsible action to sustain them, complex societies and cultures such as ours could never have come into being (been created).

Many quite different world-pictures have been created in the diverse social settings of humanity's long history. At first these pictures must have been quite simple, confined largely to the local environment. But as more complex civilizations emerged, more comprehensive pictures appeared, with speculative images and thoughts about the heavens above, the earth underfoot, and the powers that rule the world—those destructive powers that must be avoided as well as those creative and healing powers that can bring peace and health and joy. In most societies such world-pictures have been quite comprehensive: they not only displayed how things are in the world; they also set out the deep values and meanings that enable humans to orient themselves in life—enable them to find their way through moments of failure and despair as well as times of fulfillment and joy. These important features bearing on the meaning of life—what we might call the "religious dimensions" of traditional world-pictures—have, however, become desiccated and weakened in today's highly secularized pluralistic societies. This is partly because the inherited religious institutions, which have always put their emphasis on the importance of tradition, have found it difficult to adjust themselves to the increasingly rapid pace of change in today's world.

Recently, what can be called a "scientific world-picture"—beginning with the Big Bang and including a universe fourteen billion light-years across—has been imaginatively created and widely accepted (in educated circles in the West and elsewhere) as the overall context within which human life has come into being. It was in connection with this new world-picture—largely based on findings and speculations of modern astrophysics, cosmology, biology, and evolutionary theory, and increasingly becoming transcultural—that I worked out the theological position elaborated in my recent book on God as creativity (Kaufman 2004). This world-picture is often presented in the popular press as offering little explicit guidance on how humans should order their lives; and it may be touted as a picture that thoroughly refutes and undermines traditional religious views about life and the world—the alleged "warfare of science with theology" (White 1993). In my book on God as creativity and in this book on Jesus and Creativity, I am trying to move beyond that dead end by showing that, with some significant revisions, the two central symbols of Christian faith—God (creativity) and Jesus—can be brought into significant relation to this modern world-picture.[17]

IV

We can sum up this exploration of human agency—in its interconnectedness with our creativity and historicity, and its dependence on a picture of the context within which life is to be lived responsibly—by brief consideration of a value deeply cherished in many cultures today: human *freedom*.[18] As we have seen, human action becomes possible only within contexts of extraordinary complexity, including feedback inter-connections in self and society and the necessary physiological and physical supports for these; learned patterns of behavior and symbolic facility, together with correlated social customs, roles, and institutions; and subjective feelings and moods, attitudes and beliefs, pictures and knowledges of the world within which life is to be lived. Given this complex interconnected conditioning of our every action, what does it mean to speak of human groups and individuals as *free*, as in a signifi-cant sense self-determining?

It would be a mistake to regard free acts (that is, acts thought of as freely chosen) as simply *spontaneous* in origin, that is, as just beginning on their own, so to speak, as coming from nowhere. Free action emerges within a context of ongoing processes of activity and striving in an organism that is itself interconnected with ongoing sociocultural pro-cesses. To consciously and deliberately guide and order (to some extent) certain of these processes, to turn them in directions they otherwise would not go, is an emergent capacity gradually acquired, ordinarily in childhood. Dynamisms are already present and working in these vari-ous processes, as the child's freedom begins to appear; and these provide the materials and the power to which the child learns to give form and direction. As language is acquired, the child is enabled to employ more complex forms of symbolization, and this in turn makes possible envis-aging diverse sorts of potential actions with increasing accuracy and sharpness. The possibility of comparing and choosing among alterna-tives also arises. None of this could happen, of course, until humanity itself had progressed through the long linguistic-cultural-historical development we have been examining; free action and its scope and range are products of this historico-cultural process. In some cultural contexts these possibilities remain small. In others that provide the necessary patterns of social differentiation and organization together with adequate resources for symbolization, they may become highly developed. As appropriate behavioral habits and symbolization net-works, together with the requisite motor skills, are formed in the child, possibilities for acting with some measure of freedom begin to appear.

The child disciplines its fingers and learns to read music, for example, and gradually becomes able to play the piano—and thus the possibility of *choosing* to play Chopin emerges (is created). Psychological studies suggest that the childhood environments that are most conducive to the development of free and responsible agent-selves are those in which caring and love, acceptance and approval, trust and loyalty—these and other *moral* qualities!—are frequently experienced. In contrast, contexts of neglect, rejection, hatred, and violence frequently bring forth warped and stunted selves, often incapable of effective and responsible action. Thus, even in its most intensely subjective and personal dimensions, freedom is not something belonging simply to individuals. It is interpersonal and social in its origins, and it requires an appropriate social and interpersonal context for its continuing exercise and nurturance.

Freedom should not be thought of as a kind of "metaphysical" quality, a controversial matter about something humans may or may not possess. The term "freedom" refers to that which distinguishes human *action* from mere behavior; it points to those situations and those respects in which we are in a significant degree *agents*, not just organisms; it indicates that we men and women have control (in certain respects) over what we do, and that we can therefore take responsibility for it and be held accountable for it. Human agency—freedom—emerged over many generations as a gradual modification of what had originally been simply organic patterns of behavior into patterns largely humanly created and thus susceptible (to some extent) to being deliberately chosen. Our actions always remain a modification of previously existing appetites, habits, and customs over which some degree of deliberate control has been gained. They are an expression of their organic base (at least in part), the habitual and customary patterns characteristic of our sociocultural environment, and the modes of symbolization made possible by the linguistic resources available; hence, they never are "absolutely free" (whatever that might mean). My freedom thus belongs (as much) to the *context* of my action—the relationships in which I stand—as it does to me. Although freedom is a distinctive mark of our humanity, there are great disparities in the degrees to which different humans, or groups of humans, are enabled to exercise their freedom; and it is this, of course, that has informed and motivated the many recent liberation movements. This valuing of freedom goes back many centuries, and the early Christian movement made it a central theme: "For freedom Christ has set us free," declared Paul; "stand firm, therefore, and do not submit again to a yoke of slavery" (Gal. 5:1).

Up to this point I have been using the idea of deliberate choice among alternative possibilities as the principal metaphor for understanding freedom; but however illuminating that may be, it does not yet show clearly the full reach of human freedom. Our freedom is not only a matter of our ability to choose moment by moment what we will do: it is also the power to act upon and to transform our very selves. All types of self-discipline, of training the self to do something or be something—developing a skill, practicing various sorts of exercises, reading, studying, meditating—are actions of the self on itself. (Note once again the circle of self-reflexiveness that is involved here.) Such activities are usually intended to transform the self into an agent with possibilities of action different from those that now obtain—thus *creating* a somewhat new and different self. Agency is not a static condition that simply is what it is: agency is, rather, a living process, a *creative* process continuously engaged as much in transformation of itself—of opening one's self to new and different possibilities of action—as in transformation of external realities. By virtue of this power of acting upon ourselves, we are able to take responsibility not only for our particular choices and actions but—in certain respects—for our very selfhood, for what we have become and what we shall become. It was this modality of freedom of which Paul was speaking in the above quotation: the freedom to become a "new creation" (2 Cor. 5:17), the new fulfilling freedom that a re-creation "in Christ" could bring. Elsewhere he makes clear that we ourselves must take major responsibility for this transformation: "Work out your own salvation with fear and trembling," he says; "for it is God [creativity!] who is at work in you, enabling you both to will and to work for his good pleasure" (Phil. 2:12b-13).

Our consideration here of human action and responsibility, of human freedom and creativity, has brought us to some of our most profound moral—indeed religious—concerns: questions about who or what we humans are, questions about our self-acceptance and self-discipline, questions about how we should act and what goals we should pursue, questions about our failures and guilt, questions about the meaning of life, questions about the world within which we take ourselves to be living, questions about the ultimate reality with which we must come to terms. Morality and religion, it is now clear, are not peripheral or optional matters superimposed on our basic human existence, matters that we can take or leave as we like. They are matters that emerge unavoidably out of our still-developing humanity, out of our historicity, agency, and creativity—matters that emerge because we are in a significant measure free and responsible and creative. In emphasizing the appropriateness of the term "freedom" to characterize the distinctiveness of our humanity, I am not making a primarily psychological point—that we humans *feel* free in our action. Our freedom is a feature of our human self-reflexiveness; that is, of our having learned to relate ourselves not only to those others with whom we are interacting but to ourselves as well. If our freedom ever reaches its potential and we are enabled to act with a full ecological consciousness, we should find ourselves able to fit more smoothly and effectively into the natural environment that is the setting for our lives and our activities. Perhaps—in some distant future—it may even become possible for humans to feel truly at home in the world in which we find ourselves. We are, of course, far from realizing this eschatological dream. But we have tasted enough of human agency and freedom, and we know enough about what constitutes human responsibility, to have some sense of what it might mean to live as members of communities of truly free persons—at home in the world. It was an early version of this sort of vision that was expressed in the ancient metaphor of the coming "kingdom of God": Jesus—and many others during the last two thousand years—have prayed that this kingdom might come "on earth as it is in heaven." For most versions of Christian faith, Jesus has been regarded as key to the coming on planet Earth of this New Age. Chapter 4 will explore this claim that the creativity of Jesus will (or can) help bring humanity into a New Age.

As I have been arguing throughout this book, today we live in a much different world than the earliest Christians did, indeed different from that of the generations up to and including the nineteenth century. Many today, of course, do not accept the overall scientific picture of the origins of the world and of life. In my opinion, however, that picture provides us with the best information available on these matters today, though it is in many respects incomplete and will, no doubt, be modified and probably significantly transformed in future years. But its principal outlines will likely remain with us for a long time, and we can expect human life to be increasingly understood in terms of these scientific knowledges. In consequence, our understanding of many of the problems of life—as well as the overall meaning of human existence—will have to take these knowledges into account. Think of the enormous impact modern medicine and biology are already having on the way many today understand human existence and the issues with which humans now must come to terms.

It is very important that we overcome the so-called warfare of science and religion and bring our thinking about religious and moral issues into connection with our scientific knowledges. The biohistorical understanding of the human sketched in this chapter enables us, on the one hand, to maintain significant connections with modern scientific conceptions of the world around us and the web of life of which we are a part, while, on the other hand, also giving us—in the concept of human historicity—a way to connect these scientific ideas with the religious and moral themes of human freedom, creativity, and responsibility, themes of central importance to ongoing human life and its meaning. With this understanding of the complexity and the uniqueness of our humanness in place, we are in a position to sum up and assess the significance of the Jesus-trajectory$_2$ christology that began to emerge in the first two chapters of this book.

chapter four

Creativity Is *Good News!*

The early Christian message was a *gospel*, the good news that the creator of the heavens and the earth, the ruler of the universe, had sent his son to the earth in order to save humankind from all the sin, suffering, and other evils into which they had fallen. As the Gospel of John puts it: "God so loved the world that he gave his only Son, so that everyone who believes in him may not perish but may have eternal life" (3:16). That was good news for those people who first heard it, and it has remained good news for many down through the centuries. The creator and ruler of the universe loves us humans and has made the highest sacrifice to redeem human life from all evils and bring humankind into the perfect divine kingdom for which it was created. It is hardly surprising that once this gospel caught on, it spread throughout the Roman Empire and beyond. In the early decades, as we have seen, it gave rise to new visions of what human life was all about and to a new conception of God. Over the many following centuries, it spawned magnificent music and art; it stimulated profound philosophical, theological, and moral reflection; and it was a seedbed for the emergence and development of modern democratic politics and the modern sciences. All of this creativity was a product, at least in part, of Jesus-trajectory$_1$; the appearance of that trajectory proved to be an enormously creative event. There were, of course, breakdowns and failures of many sorts over the years: betrayals of the faith confessed by the churches and their leaders; crusades and murderous wars, plagues and famines, the horrors of modern slavery; Western colonialism along with Christian triumphalism; and so on and so on. But through it all the loving God was believed to be ruling from on high, and all would ultimately be good for his children on earth, if not in this life then in the next.

This good news, originally preached by the disciples and reiterated down through the centuries, was, first, that there is an *other world* than the one in which we humans now find ourselves, the heavenly world where God's perfect rule assures happiness and peace for all; and second, that God sent his son to the earth to rescue us humans, no matter how broken our lives might be, thus giving us access through Jesus to that heavenly abode. But for those of us today, for whom there is no "other world" than this one in which we find ourselves, this kind of "good news"—though a lovely dream, plausible for many centuries—can no longer provide an adequate focus for the orientation and ordering of life. Though we all sing Christmas carols rejoicing in the birth of baby Jesus, most of us know in our hearts that this beautiful story—a magnificent creation of the human imagination—is too simple and too implausible to be much of a guide to living in the world in which we today find ourselves.

Many persons, therefore—including many who think of themselves as Christians—no longer take seriously the good news of the original Christian message. What then can take its place? There is a price to pay in comfort and the hope of wish-fulfillment when we give up the anthropomorphic/anthropocentric God that we have inherited. In exchange for that price, however, there is available to us an understanding of God as *creativity*, a creativity that is real, not just an imaginary dream. It is a creativity manifest on all sides around us and present in and with our own human creativity. We humans are deeply indebted to this creativity that—through a long, precarious passage—has brought our human trajectory (and us along with it) into being. This realization gives us a basis for the hope that our trajectory—despite all failures in past and present—might continue on toward a more humane and ecologically sustainable world. Moreover, though the supernatural aspects of the traditional Jesus-story are no longer plausible, another story of the significance of Jesus still remains: the story recounted in Jesus-trajectory$_2$ can be quite meaningful for contemporary Christian faith. In this book I have been sketching an understanding of today's world in which each of the two central Christian symbols—God (understood as serendipitous creativity) and Jesus (as set out in Jesus-trajectory$_2$)—have an important place. It should be noted, however, that the "abundant life" (John 10:10) that this Jesus can bring to women and men today will be of a different sort than that expected by many earlier generations.

This understanding of Christian faith (like many earlier versions) requires a profound *conversion* to a way of living introduced to us by the image/story of Jesus, and those who make a serious commitment to this Jesus are still offered the "good news" of hope for a better human world. But instead of proffering a heavenly reward in an afterlife, this understanding offers the satisfaction of living out our years entirely within this world in which we find ourselves—with all its problems and pain, tragedy and suffering—a life to be lived within a community of love and forgiveness and hope, of reconciliation and healing and joy. It is a life given over to building new communities of peace and justice and well-being for all, a life devoted to protecting and enhancing the environment that sustains humans and many other species here on planet Earth—a this-worldly kind of "abundant life."

I

Let us review the story of Jesus as recounted in Jesus-trajectory$_2$. It begins with the ministry and message of Jesus of Nazareth, a remarkably gifted man. He was a healer, a preacher, an excellent story-teller—one who believed the end of the world (as he and his friends knew it) was coming soon, as the kingdom of God takes over from on high. Some began to believe he might be God's messiah who would overthrow the Romans and inaugurate God's kingdom on earth. Many of his stories—vivid parables recounting situations quite familiar to all his hearers but each making a distinctive point about the coming king-ship of God—were long remembered and eventually recorded in the New Testament Gospels. His sermons were sprinkled with teachings about God's love for humankind, especially the poor, the sick, and the outcast; and he called for similar love and forgiveness among humans.

Some of his teachings—as recorded in the Gospels—were very radical and quite puzzling, especially to those who thought he might be preparing to overthrow the Romans:

> "You have heard that it was said, 'An eye for an eye and a tooth for a tooth.' But I say to you, Do not resist an evildoer. But if anyone strikes you on the right cheek, turn the other also; and if anyone wants to sue you and take your coat, give your cloak as well. . . .
> "You have heard that it was said, 'You shall love your neighbor and hate your enemy.' But I say to you, Love your enemies and pray for those who persecute you, so that you may be children of your Father in heaven." (Matt. 5:38-40, 43-45)

Jesus was obviously a very creative charismatic person, a great exorcist and healer, and he attracted considerable attention wherever he went in Palestine. When the Jewish and Roman authorities arrested him as a troublemaker who might be planning an insurrection, he—in keeping with his teachings—made no effort to resist. And when one of his disciples "put his hand on his sword, drew it, and struck the slave of the high priest, cutting off his ear. . . . Jesus said to him, 'Put your sword back into its place; for all who take the sword will perish by the sword'" (Matt. 26:51-52). After being questioned by the Jewish authorities and Pilate, he was crucified. And that should have been the end of the story and the end of his influence in human affairs: one more death of a creative innocent man.

But that event was, in fact, not the end of the story of Jesus but instead the beginning of a new and quite different sequence of events with, as it turned out, enormously *creative* consequences of a sort not expected by anyone. Had these strange events—quite difficult even to imagine—not occurred, we today would never have heard of Jesus, his ministry and his comportment in life, his death, his provocative teachings. After Jesus' death and burial some of his disciples began to speak of his continuing appearances to them, and they (and others) came to believe he was alive again: God had resurrected him from the dead and through him had begun inaugurating his kingdom on earth. A new story about Jesus was being created. It soon began to spread rapidly, and the Jesus-movement grew, incorporating many Gentiles as well as Jews.

This alone might have been of significant historical importance, but the creativity in this movement was not limited simply to growth in size: over the next decades it also produced substantial rethinking of who or what God really is and what God requires of humans, how humans are to live. These significantly transformative changes were summed up compactly toward the end of the first century c.e. by the writer of 1 John:

> Beloved, let us love one another, because love is from God; everyone who loves is born of God and knows God. Whoever does not love does not know God, for *God is love*. God's love was revealed among us in this way: God sent his only Son into the world so that we might live through him. . . . No one has ever seen God; if we love one another, God lives in us, and his love is perfected in us. (4:7-9, 12; emphasis added)

Christology is the area of Christian thinking that deals with the understanding of Jesus—Jesus as a human being and Jesus' special relationship to God. In this book I am developing a christology that is in keeping with the interpretation of God as *creativity*. After briefly sketching in chapter 1 a conception of Jesus as thoroughly human in all respects (a central emphasis of Jesus-trajectory$_2$), I presented an outline, in chapter 2, of Jesus' *normativity* for today, his normativity for our human existence and also for our understanding of God—that is, our understanding of *creativity*. Creativity is not to be thought of any longer as simply the bringing into being of just anything and everything. However true that vague and general definition might be, those groups and individuals who regard Jesus as providing normative meaning for human life have reason to take the image/story of Jesus as bearing significantly on their understanding of creativity. As the disciples sought to make sense of what they called the resurrection of Jesus, it gradually became clear to them that in and through Jesus, God—or in our terms, *creativity*—was doing something new and decisively different from what had been understood in the past: a new vision of what the human strand of life was all about, and what it might become, was being created.[1] Moreover, this vision was so strikingly different from what had previously been taken for granted about human life and its possibilities that it implied God (creativity) also must be significantly different from what had previously been understood. During the first Christian century (as discussed in chapters 1 and 2) a great change took place in the conception of God held by at least some of Jesus' followers. They began preaching this gospel to all who would listen, and they themselves sought to live out the new pattern of life that the gospel called for. They believed they stood in a distinctive, indeed unique, relationship to God: they were the vehicle through which this "new creation" (as Paul put it) was coming into being. To put this in our twenty-first-century language: they believed that the creativity on planet Earth, the creativity (God) that had brought forth life in general and later on human life, had also brought forth Jesus of Nazareth and his ministry and message of love, forgiveness, and redemption. And it was to this further creativity (this act of God) that Jesus' disciples and other followers believed they were responding as they spread this gospel and lived out this new life of love wherever they went. Many Christians over the centuries have also heard this call by God and responded affirmatively to it. All of this (as we noted in chapter 2) tells us something about creativity (God) that we would otherwise not know. It tells us that creativity is not just a vague and general appearance of something new and transformative, anywhere and everywhere: it may also manifest itself in and through events as specific and distinctive as the image and story of Jesus.

We need to consider further now what can be said about Jesus and creativity. Three distinctly different points can be made. There was Jesus' own creativity in his ministry, healings, and teachings; then there was also the amazing creativity that occurred after his death: first the resurrection appearances of Jesus, and following on these the several decades of reconceiving—in decisively new ways—God, the kingship of God, and how humans were to live out their lives; finally, there has been the striving by committed followers of Jesus over the centuries to live within this new creative pattern of human life, a mode of creativity continuing all the way down into the present. We know very little about how all this creativity got under way. With respect to the creativity of Jesus before his death, there was of course the influence of John the Baptizer in the desert and Jesus' joining John's company of disciples, as well as the fertile consequences of Jesus' own strong hope and expectation that God was about to bring in (or was already bringing in) a New Age. With respect to the creativity immediately following upon Jesus' death, we can say a few things, but it is all very murky. Obviously, the vivid memories of Jesus' ministry, death, and teachings, and the disciples' great disappointment following his crucifixion, must have been important factors. But we can only speculate about how these were related to the resurrection appearances, which then led to the disciples' creative attempts to understand the meaning of Jesus' crucifixion and resurrection, and eventually to the strikingly new vision of God as love, as well as to the missions that spread abroad that remarkable message. The powerful ongoing historical momentum of the Jesus-movement, a momentum still under way, was thus coming into being.

The most important evidence of this new creative thinking of the disciples is found largely in the Pauline and Johannine documents in the New Testament. But the earliest of these, some of Paul's writings, were not written until about a generation after Jesus' death; and Paul must have had important creative predecessors about whom we know little. The Johannine texts were produced much later, probably toward the end of the first century c.e., or even after that. By the end of that century, the story of Jesus was on its way to becoming a worldwide phenomenon. Jesus was going to be one of the most influential figures of history, one whose story would continue to transform lives creatively, one who would inspire religious and cultural creativity of many sorts. An enormous stream of human social, cultural, artistic, and intellectual creativity has followed upon his life, death, and resurrection. (Perhaps the only comparable examples have been the creativity that followed upon the lives of the Buddha and Mohammed.) Human existence around the world has obviously been greatly enriched by this Jesus-stream of creativity. It must be granted, however, that this creativity has also been the fountain of some very destructive historical movements and events: one thinks of the long history of Christian intolerance of other religions (as well as of other Christians, in all too many cases!), and especially of the anti-Semitism during much of Christian history, culminating in the Holocaust of the twentieth century. One thinks also of the patriarchal oppression of women throughout Christian history; of the Crusades, the Inquisition, the slave trade, modern colonialism, and modern mass warfare carried on by each side in the names of Jesus and/or God; and so on. Today we live in a historical period in which there is still a very wide Jesus-stream, but the *ambiguity* of that stream's creativity is obvious.

There are, of course, many churchgoers who are basically nominal Christians but who do not let their religion interfere with "the good life"—a frenetic pursuit of "American values," such as a "high standard of living" with plenty of money, entertainment, and other pleasures. The creativity to be found in this stance would seem to have little connection with Jesus. Then there are those far-right Christian fundamentalists (especially in the United States) who seem to be all too creative in their willingness to use almost any kind of instrumentalities (including mass media brouhaha, political "dirty tricks" of many different sorts, some forms of "brainwashing," even modern warfare) as they spread their version of "the Gospel" and combat those they regard as "God's enemies" (atheists, secularists, Jews, Muslims, and many others—including other Christians) in their effort to create a "Christian America." And there are faithful ordinary Christians for whom Jesus presents the most compelling model of how we humans ought to live, but—finding it impossible to order their lives in terms of his extreme demands—who are simply good, decent people. Then there are those who seek to order their lives by creatively responding to Jesus' most *radical* teachings about love, caring for the poor and needy, and practicing forgiveness, reconciliation, and peacemaking. And there are those who think that although one ought to lead one's *personal* life in terms of the radical teachings about forgiveness and love, these teachings do not apply to the wider social and political order. There are those who are convinced that Jesus' teachings require us to create a new social, political, and economic order in which all will be cared for in justice and peace. And so on and so on. The Jesus-stream has long since lost its creative cutting edge—or perhaps it would be more accurate to say it has spawned many quite different cutting edges, in confusing contradiction with each other—and it is hard to know just what we should make of this enormous ambiguity.

Some may think it is time to acknowledge that Jesus can no longer help us much, either in identifying the problems with which we humans must today come to terms or through inspiring creative address to those problems. But where else should we turn for truly creative inspiration? It is clear that the radicality of Jesus' preaching and teaching (as we find it in the New Testament) simply cannot be lived out in any legalistic way—and this accounts for some of the diversity and ambiguity just noted in the many different responses to Jesus in today's world. But it should also be clear that the radicality of Jesus' demands may startle our minds into fresh thinking about how we humans need to reorder our lives and our world.[2] Perhaps only a powerful dramatic vision of what human life can and should be—such as Jesus' radical vision of life under God's kingship—is capable of inspiring us to break through today's barriers and create new forms of human existence. Jesus' *radicality*, that is to say, may still inspire us to strive toward creating a new and better world. And for just this reason, it seems to me, it is precisely this radicality of Jesus to which Christians should be attending as they seek to move creatively into what will undoubtedly be a complex and difficult future. Other Christians, of course, may feel there are good reasons to opt for other features of the Jesus-story. And non-Christians would likely move in some entirely different directions as they seek creative ways to identify and address the major problems to which we humans today must direct our energies—though doubtless some who do not claim to be Christian at all might (as has often been the case) continue to turn toward the radical Jesus for inspiration.

It is not obvious that the Jesus-stream in the contemporary world still has the resources either to identify or to creatively address the major problems that we humans are increasingly facing as we become a single, highly interdependent—though still quite pluralistic—humanity. Can Christian churches find ways—other than the exercise of dominative power (which they have not hesitated to employ in the past)—to help bring a new creative peace and order into today's pluralism, with its many divisive socio-cultural dimensions? Can the Christian spirit find sufficient inspiration—in its notes of nonviolent and nonresistant love even of enemies—to put aside its idolatrous claims to be the sole truly redemptive force in human history? Can it learn to rejoice in the creativity manifest in other religious and secular movements and begin to work more cooperatively with them? Can Christians—moving beyond their traditional anthropomorphic/anthropocentric god, and standing in awe of the creativity (God!) manifest throughout the universe as well as in human affairs—begin to order their activities more fully in terms of what will be good for all of life on planet Earth, not simply human life? All Christians who commit themselves to versions of the Jesus image/story that emphasize what I have called the *radical* character of his vision and message would, I hope, be able to say yes to all of these questions.

II

In chapter 3 we explored briefly the understanding of humans as fundamentally *biohistorical* beings, a conception that enables us to connect such valued features of human existence as agency, creativity, freedom, and love with our complex biological and historical grounding. Obviously, we are *biological* beings, products of a long evolutionary development of life here on planet Earth, but we are not ordinary animals. We are "incomplete or unfinished animals" (Geertz),[3] which, through a long, slow process of emergence from our biological origins, have become beings who cannot survive unless we are "completed" by the humanly created cultures into which we have been born. As beings created in part by the sociocultural setting in which we have grown up, we have acquired capacities to act self-consciously, responsibly, and creatively, and we are thus able to participate actively in the transformation of our biohistorical world. Though we have been decisively shaped, and continue to be nourished, by the biological and sociohistorical *pasts* from which we and our forebears have come, it is the problems confronting us in the *present* with which we must come to terms, if human life is to continue and to flourish in the *future* ahead of us. Past, present, and future are bound together in our lives, each playing its own distinctive part in our biohistorical existence. Today our local sociocultural worlds are changing very rapidly as a global society is coming into being, and there are many enormous problems that need to be addressed.

The picture of our human situation that I have been presenting here is a naturalistic/humanistic one. In this picture there is no creator-God on high ruling all of these developments, a God we can be confident is bringing humanity to a glorious final consummation. But it is not the case, either, that the predicaments we humans face will be overcome simply by our *human* decisions and actions. A mysterious *creativity* (God) has been manifest throughout the universe all the way back to the very beginning of things.[4] And the human biohistorical trajectory was a serendipitous product of this creativity; we humans did not create the world in which we find ourselves, nor did we create ourselves. Our forebears, however, gradually began to play a role in the creativity through which humanity emerged from ordinary animality, as the mysterious creativity in the universe brought into being a human offshoot (so to speak).[5] For many generations this specifically *human* role in these creative developments—though gradually increasing in significance—was very small. By several millennia ago, however, human creativity was playing an important part, and in the modern era it has had a significant role in the creative transformation of both human existence and the surface of the earth. The wider creativity manifest throughout the universe—God—has, of course, always had the larger part in these matters: certainly the fundamentally biohistorical character of human existence, as well as its happening here on planet Earth, was not the result simply of human decisions and actions. What the future will bring is, very likely, partly in our hands; but the final outcome (unless we destroy ourselves, which now seems possible) is not in our hands at all. Ultimately, thus, we must put our trust in that wider creativity—deeply mysterious, but also surprisingly beneficent—as we humans play out our own creative role in addressing the problems we face.

This, of course, is how it has always been with *God*. Faith in God was born initially in ancient Israel, as the Israelites came to believe that what God (Yahweh) had done for them in the past—especially in the escape from Egypt and the invasion of Canaan—provided grounds for hope about what he would do in the future. Despite this hope, however, what God was believed to be actually doing always turned out to be in many respects quite unpredictable and incomprehensible—a profound *mystery*. The situation remains the same today. The human story and its context to date (as we now understand these) can provide grounds for hope respecting the future: from its very beginning this story is about a trajectory of *serendipitous creativity* and its effects—a creativity that was deeply beneficial to the gradually emerging human life. This creativity made possible both the emergence of humans and their distinctive development. As we look backward down our human trajectory, we can see that the creativity working in and through these evolutionary and historical processes did not move forward every which way; rather, it built upon what was already in place, extending it and expanding it as it moved on into the future. That is, this creativity *adapts* itself, so to speak, to the possibilities for growth and development in each new stage, and this enables the trajectory to move onward. (Without this adjustment, the trajectory might well die.) Even though this has been a long, slow evolutionary-historical development requiring hundreds of thousands of years and much tragedy and pain, it can still provide a basis for hope that the creativity here on planet Earth will continue opening up new possibilities for the human trajectory as it moves on into the future. We can and should place our confidence respecting that future in this ongoing creativity—this creativity that, as I have been arguing, we should understand to be God.

It is difficult for us to grasp all that is involved in this sort of judgment unless we bracket our ordinary human timescale—measured basically in days and years and generations—and think in much larger terms.[6] The creation of the new in the world often comes quite slowly, and it was only through very gradual changes that the emergence of humankind, as we know it, came about. It was, for example, a considerable achievement—taking many generations to accomplish—for emerging *Homo sapiens* to begin taking into account the most minimal of *moral* considerations, such as rules restricting vengeance. We find such a rule in Exodus, shortly after a summary of the Ten Commandments: "You shall give life for life, eye for eye, tooth for tooth, hand for hand, foot for foot" (21:23b-24). This rule equalizing the punishment with the crime may seem rigid and harsh to us today; nevertheless, it represents a significant moral advance over the practice of Lamech, the father of Noah, who bragged to his wives: "I kill a man for wounding me, a young man for a blow. Cain may be avenged seven times, but Lamech seventy-seven" (Gen. 4:23b-24; 5:28-29 NEB). And it took many generations more, as can be seen from the record in the Hebrew Bible, to develop such values as mercy, justice, and kindness—strongly emphasized by the eighth-century B.C.E. prophets[7]—and to begin ordering human life by them. In other cultures, similar developments were also occurring—sometimes, of course, going in quite different directions. Even given the deep and rich moral consciousness being serendipitously created in Israel's culture, it took another eight centuries for a quite new vision to appear in the ministry and preaching of Jesus—a vision of human life ordered and oriented by love and forgiveness.

The image/story of Jesus brought forth possibilities for human existence heretofore unimagined: a vision and hope that Christians (and some others) have believed could guide humans creatively into a new future. Of course, the Jesus-story can also lead us into despair: to what extent, after all, has it really changed the human condition in the last two thousand years? I have claimed above that it has been very creative in many ways, but one cannot help but wonder whether its creativity may now be largely spent. Other historical forces clearly dominate human life today, and the major churches and movements that claim to be Christian seem to be thoroughly compromised in many respects: very little is heard these days about what I have been calling the *radical* character of the image and story of Jesus. Perhaps its time is over?

A judgment of that sort takes for granted our ordinary human time-scale, and (as we have just been noting) this may be quite misleading when considering the kind of issues with which we are here concerned. If it took thousands of years for *Homo sapiens* to move beyond bare animality and begin to acquire—to *create*—an elemental moral consciousness; and even with that new sensitivity in place, it took hundreds of years more for such basic moral ideals as justice, kindness, and mercy to become widely affirmed in cultures and religions, we should not be so surprised and disappointed that these norms are so often still violated around the world (think of recent and ongoing outbreaks of massive genocide, brutal dictatorships, wars, to say nothing of the all-too-frequent incidents of everyday ordinary meanness). We need to remember that our basic human physiology, after all—including our limbic system, nervous system, and brain—was formed in times when humans had to fight for their lives against ferocious predators (see, e.g., Ehrenreich 1997 and Ashbrook and Albright 1997). That underlying equipment is still with us, along with—in nearly every culture—practices, traditions, and institutions that encourage violent aggression against, and violent responses to, enemies believed to be threatening. Human morality has to temper, tame, and discipline all of this in each new generation; so it should not be surprising that progress toward cultures of reconciliation, peace, and goodwill has been painfully slow and with many reversals. It is difficult for us humans to sustain even such obviously wise ordinary moral standards as the ones just mentioned. Why would anyone expect, then, that the radical vision of Jesus ought to be taken seriously? It is clearly an impossible dream.

But perhaps the time for that impossible dream has come. We humans are today in a different situation than we have ever been before. This new situation was ushered in at the end of World War II with the dropping of the atomic bomb on Hiroshima. Theologian Henry Nelson Wieman realized almost immediately that for the first time in history humans had available a kind of power that could bring the human story to an end, and this meant that the human situation on Earth had changed decisively:

> The bomb that fell on Hiroshima cut history in two like a knife. Before and after are two different worlds. That cut is more abrupt, decisive, and revolutionary than the cut made by the star over Bethlehem ... more swiftly transformative of human existence than anything else that has ever happened. The economic and political order fitted to the age before that parachute fell becomes suicidal in the age coming after. The same breach extends into education and religion. (Wieman 1946:37)

For the next few decades—with stores of atomic implements of war building up on both sides of the Iron Curtain—there were worldwide fears that we humans might be about to destroy ourselves. But what we were actually doing during that period was learning a precarious way to live with our newfound weapons. Now, sixty years after Hiroshima and with the "cold war" decades behind us, we continue to worry about atomic weapons. Moreover, though we have learned to take the bomb for granted, another new situation—much more difficult to manage—is increasingly coming to our attention (though many in high positions in the United States are unwilling to acknowledge it): we are in the midst of an ecological crisis. Like the danger of nuclear war, it is a crisis very likely brought on largely by our own behavior: our population growth on planet Earth, our wasteful use of energy and other resources to power our "high" standard of living in North America and Europe, our unthinking destruction of the habitat of many species of life that are as a result becoming extinct, our contribution to the global warming that is rapidly changing our moderate climate, and so on. Above all in this list, we must note our own unwillingness to discipline ourselves sufficiently to address these and many other ecological problems in an effective way.

The dangers of environmental breakdown to ongoing human life are not new. They have been a factor throughout human history, and failure to adjust human activities intelligently to environmental changes has often been a major factor in the collapse of civilizations in the past (see Diamond 2005). But heretofore these were always *local* failures, and the human project was able to continue because it was carried on elsewhere. Today we are facing *worldwide* environmental changes, at least partially caused by human failures to care properly for the environment; and there no longer are other places to which our population of six billion humans can go to continue the human story. Either we today learn how to accommodate our living to the ecological requirements around the globe, or the human story is likely to come to an end.

None of the great world religions anticipated this state of affairs: that we humans would at some time have the power to destroy the entire human project, and that we might exercise that power. So Wieman was correct that in the middle of the last century we humans moved into a completely unprecedented (and unexpected) historical situation. In these circumstances what is needed above all is truly *imaginative* creativity. Actually, this is the kind of creativity that we humans possess. There is no reason to expect that the wider creativity manifest throughout the universe (God) will intervene here in our behalf (as may be hoped by some devotees of the traditional anthropocentric God); as far as we know, this is not the way in which that creativity happens. Our *human* creativity, however—alone in the universe in this respect?—can be guided to some degree by our human imaginings, our human desires, our human intentions. The dilemma with which we are here concerned is one that we humans have (unexpectedly) produced as we enthusiastically exercised our own increasingly developing creativity and power—and we are the ones who must address it.

So what is now required of us humans most of all is (1) creativity, *imaginative* creativity deliberately directed toward addressing this very dangerous situation; and (2) the moral and political will to hasten disarmament (nuclear and otherwise) and take whatever steps are necessary to reverse our growing environmental destruction. This is a large and difficult agenda, an agenda politically quite unpopular, at least here in the United States—the worst offender in the world on these matters. In this country today we do not seem to have in our culture and political leadership—or in our religious consciousness—either the moral resources or the imagination to grasp the enormity of this problem. We are myopic lemmings running toward the sea as we spread the gospel of corporate capitalism around the globe and (mis)manage affairs at home with a politics of fear. And instead of seeking to understand and appreciate cultures and religions and languages different from our own, we put our hope in a Fortress America that will keep out poverty-driven people led by "evil terrorists."

There may, however, be an ironic feature in this picture. We are living in the midst of a new globalism that is breaking down isolationist boundaries of many sorts around the world. From the time *Homo sapiens* left Africa and began to travel around the globe, humans took up abode in many different, often quite isolated, locations; and further development of the human biohistorical line occurred in each of these separate settings. Since each society and culture developed its own way to live— as it adapted itself to its geographical setting—diverse human societies, cultures, languages, religions, practices, and values were created in these different places. The human story thus became many quite distinct and separate stories. Some of these groups evolved into major civilizations; others became quite isolated and remained small. Although there have been—all the way down to the twenty-first century—many political and military attempts to bring some order into this thoroughly pluralistic situation, no empire has succeeded in bringing all these diverse groups together and ruling the world. Modern technology, however, has made possible increasing interchange among civilizations around the globe during the past several centuries; and during the last decades of the twentieth century, something truly new has begun to happen.

With the creation of the worldwide electronic Web, instantaneous moving of information of all sorts everywhere around the globe is now in place; and we are rapidly becoming one world economically, industrially, and scientifically. There is also much social interchange and cultural mixing. So the many distinct human stories in our pluralized history are becoming one overall story; it will likely remain very pluralistic and complex well into the future, but there is going to be a unified human story once again. Unfortunately, however, we remain politically divided into so-called sovereign nation-states (though the European Union is taking important steps to overcome that); and with a weak

United Nations, it is still much too easy for powerful arrogant nations to make highly destructive warfare against weaker powers. A third world war, if it should occur, would be among nations with weapons of mass destruction, and therefore might be virtually the end of the human story. If we manage to avoid such a war, we will, of course, still have the ecological crisis to deal with, so either way the human future at present looks dark.

Our most important human task today, therefore, is to see that we avoid both of these disasters. We must continue to move as rapidly as we can into one, largely democratic, political world; and we must make major progress on our environmental problems. Is there any chance for both of these to happen? It surely will not be easy, since there is not even agreement in the major civilizations that we should put these objectives high on our agendas. To make the necessary sharp turn in the roads we are presently following will require a great deal of quite *imaginative* creativity, and that right soon.

III

In short, what is needed is a worldwide conversion—a religious-like conversion!—to a new and quite different way of ordering our societies, our institutions, our cultures, our religions, our families, our individual lives. Throughout the whole long history of humankind, in all its many different sociocultural and religious strands, it has been taken for granted that we humans should largely live out of the authoritative traditions and practices of the past. We are, of course, bio*historical* beings, shaped by the past—indeed, we have been given our very humanness by the past—and in all cultures we have been taught and have learned that we must respect, honor, cherish, and pass on this past to the future. But as historical beings we are not only created and nourished by our past: we actually *live* in the *present*, and we must, therefore, come to terms with the major problems we now face if the human race is to survive into the *future* and flourish in that future. As we have noted, we have inherited powerful biohistorical momentums from our human pasts, momentums that are today driving us toward self-destruction; these must be changed. Those basic patterns of orientation in life—which divide us from each other and into groups suspicious of each other and often fighting, enemies seeking to destroy each other instead of living peacefully together in communities and societies ordered justly; and which lead us to neglect care of our environment, continuing to exploit it for our own short-term pleasures and gain—must be drastically transformed. We no longer dare to live out our lives and carry on our activities in our politics and economics, our cultures and religions, our sciences and technologies, our personal relations and friendships, in the terms largely specified by these historical momentums, however effective and valuable they may have been in the past. For we are living in a *new* present, qualitatively different from any of our human pasts, a present in which these patterns of orientation and ordering that enabled us to live and flourish throughout our long human history are now threatening to destroy us and the entire human future. Unless we change these inherited ways of living and acting, believing and hoping, we may commit species suicide. We have no alternative, therefore, (1) to learning how to live together in some kind of lasting peace and justice, in which (2) we *cooperatively* find ways to deal effectively with the ecological crisis. A massive religious-like conversion is needed.

Does this mean that we must become members of some new religion that displaces and wipes out the cherished values and meanings and standards by which our lives have heretofore been ordered? That is a self-contradictory idea, not even imaginable, for it would involve destroying what makes us human in order to make us more human. Nevertheless, it is a *religious-like* conversion that is needed, for what is called for here are changes in very deep-lying patterns that at present orient and order most of human life worldwide. They are patterns partially grounded in the biological side of our human nature, grounded in features inherited from the prehuman and early human stages of the evolutionary developments through which humanity emerged; and they are also grounded in long-standing historico-cultural patterns. From early on, of course, developments in the historical side of our humanness often involved (or led to) significant transformation of some aspects of our strictly biological inheritance;[8] and, as Sigmund Freud saw, this gave rise to major enduring tensions in human selfhood between what he called the "superego" and the "id."[9] As we noted above, it took many centuries for moral (and other) constraints on the *id* to become sufficiently effective to enable large-scale societies to emerge. And in today's world, of course, there continue to be breakdowns of many different sorts in this order. I am not suggesting here that it is necessary for the constraints of the superego to be tightened still further today—even if that could be accomplished, the consequences might be explosive. Rather, I suggest that, as is often the case in religious conversions, these constraints be creatively *transformed* into new configurations more appropriate to the situation in which humanity now finds itself.

What might these new configurations be? And how could they be brought about? I cannot give a general answer to either of these questions. That would require massive knowledge of the religio-moral and secular-humanist patterns that presently orient and order human existence around the globe, as well as proposals for transforming each of these patterns in an appropriate new direction. This important religio-cultural task—a task of worldwide proportions—needs to be undertaken from within each of the major civilizations and religio-cultural groupings that presently order humanity around the globe; it cannot be imposed from without.

Actually, however, changes of the sort we are considering here may already be getting under way serendipitously: many persons and groups in countries around the globe seem to have become aware of our ecological problems, and the problems rooted in situations of extreme poverty, and they are becoming more and more insistent that governments and other agencies take appropriate action. Worldwide conferences have been held for a number of decades, and such achievements as the Kyoto Protocol represent a beginning cooperative step forward with regard to the environmental situation—the outstanding exception to making this step being the United States. Establishment of the International Court of Justice is also a major cooperative step toward necessary legal standards for ordering world affairs. The United Nations is, of course, the major international institution—however weak it may be—that must move us forward on these matters; but other institutions such as the World Bank and the International Monetary Fund are also beginning to wake up to the need for major changes in the way international economic and ecological problems are handled. Moreover, some large worldwide corporations have obviously seen the handwriting on the wall and are attempting to mend their ways accordingly. We may hope, thus, that some beginnings of important transformations in the ways we humans have been ordering and orienting human life for hundreds of generations are already under way. There is, of course, resistance in many quarters to the decisive changes now required in our familiar patterns of ordering our affairs—defenders of "national sovereignty" being an obvious example, with advocates of international corporate capitalism a close second, and religious institutions and traditions unwilling to respect each other and work together cooperatively an important third; and we may not make the changes as rapidly as is necessary. But the worldwide *religious-like* conversion in our thinking and our feelings, about the way we humans have heretofore ordered our affairs, does appear to be under way to some extent. The creativity that brought our human trajectory into being and enabled it to go forward over many millennia is, perhaps, opening up some new possibilities as we move into the future. And it can be hoped that, as we slowly learn how to make some of these moves cooperatively, we may begin to move forward more confidently and thus more rapidly.

I am not qualified to suggest the ways in which our many religious and humanist traditions need to reorient themselves, nor can I speak for all Christians. I can, however, suggest what I think is appropriate for the version of Christian faith that I have been presenting in these pages. We are concerned here about a human world that is beginning to be forced by economic, industrial, ecological, and humanitarian forces to come together again, after being separated into distinct cultures, religions, languages, and civilizations for thousands of years. It is a world in which these disparate traditions have usually been quite suspicious of each other; have fought wars with—and often sought to completely destroy—each other; have seldom lived in any kind of deep respect for each other. All of this must now change as we become a single worldwide society—a society doubtless remaining pluralistic in many respects but in which the major groupings are increasingly interconnected and thus interdependent. If this new world is actually to be created, many of the long-standing practices, prejudices, beliefs, values, attitudes, ways of living and interacting of our nations, our cultures, our civilizations, our religions, our political institutions, our large corporations, and other social groupings must be transformed into much more cooperative and trusting patterns. For if we do not succeed in moving forward into a new global society that can effectively address the problems we humans now face, utterly destructive breakdowns may bring the whole human story to an end.

IV

I would like to suggest now what a Christian perspective and faith, of the sort to which I have been alluding, have to offer in this crucial historical moment. The kind of transformative changes needed—in our cultures, our practices, our attitudes, our institutions, our ways of living—will undoubtedly require very considerable human *creativity*. At present we do not know how to bring about these changes; we do not even know what the necessary first steps should be. New insights into the problems we face, new proposals on how to address these problems, fresh thinking and imagining of ways to proceed—in short, a new willingness to acknowledge the seriousness of our enormous problems and a new willingness to be open to radical changes in the orientation and the ordering of our inherited ways of living must all be *created*.

In the Jewish, Christian, and Muslim traditions, *creativity* has always been a central mark—indeed the *defining* mark—of God. In the theology with which we are working in this book, creativity *is* God, God *is* creativity—the creativity that has brought all that exists into being, the creativity that continues to be active throughout the universe, the creativity that has brought us humans into being and is manifest worldwide in and through our own human creativity. God-as-creativity is not to be thought of as in any respect a sectarian god, largely connected with, say, only the Abrahamic religions. The God of which I am speaking here is the creativity manifest throughout the cosmos, the creativity evident in all human practices and traditions, the ongoing coming into being of the new to be seen everywhere in the universe. When I say, then, that *creativity* will be required if we are to address effectively the worldwide problems we humans today face, it is not some parochial Western or Christian kind of creativity to which I am referring and appealing. It is the universal creativity—the coming into being of the novel and transformative wherever and whenever that happens—the creativity known of and manifest in the lives and cultures of all peoples.

It is on this creativity that our hopes for the human future should be placed. The creative changes that are needed around the world must come about in ways appropriate to each tradition and culture, not just changes that we in the Abrahamic religions or we in the West might desire and hope for. The new world that we hope to help create must be one to which peoples of all cultures, religions, and languages contribute, and in which they can all feel at home.

The creativity required to bring about this new order may well go beyond the creative inspiration we humans are able to provide: we must hope and expect and believe that the wider creativity (God) will continue to engender a context in the world roundabout that will enable us, indeed encourage us, to move forward. In view of all that this wider creativity has done for us humans—bringing us forth in the world over countless generations—it is fitting that we continue to have faith in it as we move forward into an unknown future. Doubtless as we attempt to address the large problems we humans now face, there will be many differences in our judgments about which insights we should regard as truly creative and therefore pursue; so we will need to learn how to search together for creative ways to move beyond these differences, and that will often be difficult. However, it is worth noting that throughout the whole of humanity today there appear to be serendipitous *pressures* that, after all those past centuries of divisions and separateness, are beginning to pull us humans together again in spite of ourselves. Is *God*—the creativity manifest in the wider context in which we humans live—now nudging us forward? It is important that we accede to these pressures and do everything we can to facilitate this transformation.

As we have been observing throughout these pages, the Christian message is not only about God, the wider creativity. It is also about Jesus, a very creative figure of two thousand years ago. As might be expected, those of us who are Christians will turn to the mission and message of Jesus for help in addressing the massive problems that we humans today confront, problems about which there is much disagreement. Jesus' creativity—in his ministry, his comportment, his healings, his teachings, and especially in the manner in which he went to his crucifixion—inspired those around him. And following upon his alleged resurrection from the dead, his mission and message were carried around the Roman world and beyond, and it inspired many others to become his disciples and followers—a movement that continues to grow. We Christians need to ask ourselves, Do the life and death of this Jesus in any way significantly bear on the complex of problems with which we humans must now come to terms? Does this Jesus have anything to say that might illuminate these problems in some significant way?

Jesus believed that the kingdom of God was beginning to break into human history; and he regarded his own healings of sickness and suffering, and his forgiveness of sins, as signs that this kingdom was coming soon. He believed that humans should love not only both God and their neighbors but their enemies as well, "so that you may be children of your Father in heaven" (Matt. 5:44-45). And this love was understood in a very radical sense. It required, for instance, repeatedly forgiving the offenses of others against us (according to Matt.18:22, Jesus told Peter that those who had offended him should be forgiven "seventy times seven"); going out of our way to help other human beings who are suffering (as the story of "the good Samaritan" suggests, Luke 10:29-37); going "the second mile" and turning "the other cheek" (Matt. 5:43-47). I am not suggesting that followers of Jesus are duty-bound to obey literally these prescriptions. I am suggesting that the life to which Jesus called his followers involves a *reversal* of ordinary social and political, cultural and—all too often—religious standards, according to which power over others signifies one's importance, and serving others is regarded as demeaning (Mark 10:43-44). All this was brought into sharp and unforgettable focus by the final events of Jesus' life: he refused to defend or protect himself from his enemies, and he accepted meekly the whips and curses and finally the suffering of a violent death at their hands.[10]

Jesus was obviously a very creative figure: he imagined a world decisively different from the one he lived in—this present world governed by relations of power and violence, this world of injustice, disease, and ugliness; and he announced that this new world of reconciliation, love, and peace was soon coming here on Earth. And so, in keeping with that expectation, he called for new and quite different human behaviors— even in this present world—behaviors driven by a love that sacrifices itself without reservation to the needs of others; that ministers to the sick, the weak, the poor; that refuses to fight back against those who have done harm but instead forgives.

This vision of the possibilities of human beings—of the potentiality of humankind—is certainly one of the most radical ever set forth. Jesus' belief, and his enactment of that belief in his own life and death—that human existence should (and could!) at all points radiate *agape*-love—captivated his followers and powerfully motivated them to change their lives. Virtually every writer in the New Testament affirms the importance of love in one way or another. Paul and John, the two great theologians of the New Testament, both emphasized love's centrality and its glory: Paul, especially in his great hymn to love in 1 Corinthians 13, in which he very straightforwardly affirms that of the three basic Christian virtues—faith, hope, and love—"the greatest of these is love" (13:13); a Johannine writer, especially in his daring pronouncement that "God is love, and those who abide in love abide in God, and God abides in them" (1 John 4:16). This radical vision of the human potential may help us see more clearly what will be required if we are to move past the hatreds and aggressiveness, the misplaced loyalties, the defensive ideas of duty and honor and patriotism, and the like, to an openness that welcomes other peoples, cultures, and religions; and a willingness to forgive and forget past injuries and crimes. The radical love and forgiveness advocated by Jesus can transform destructive human practices and lives, thus helping to break down long-standing barriers of hatred and fear that make it impossible for peoples and nations, ethnic and religious groups, to live together and work together cooperatively for a better human world. The apostle Paul had something like this in mind when he laid out his vision of the meaning and power of love: "Love is patient; love is kind; love is not envious or boastful or arrogant or rude. It does not insist on its own way; it is not irritable or resentful; it . . . rejoices in the truth. It bears all things, believes all things, hopes all things, endures all things. Love never ends" (1 Cor. 13:4-8). Christians were being transformed by this gospel of love, and they had been given the commission to spread it around the world. It was because of the transformative power of this love that Paul was able to declare that "if anyone is in Christ, there is a new creation: everything . . . has become new! All this is from God" (2 Cor. 5:17-18).

In the New Testament, of course, this vision of humankind's potential presupposed a supernaturalistic world-picture: God was doing all these things in connection with bringing human history to its climax and goal, the perfect kingdom of God in and over the human world. Perhaps only in a context of this sort could such an implausible vision of the human potential ever have been created—human existence being what, for the most part, it has been. However that may be, as new generations of Christians came and went, and it became increasingly apparent that the apocalyptic expectations of Jesus, Paul, and the others simply were not happening as anticipated, the new vision of the possibilities of human existence as a life of "love, joy, peace, patience, kindness, generosity, faithfulness, gentleness, and self-control" (as Paul described it in his letter to the Galatians, 5:22-23) did not die away. Instead, it became the hoped-for quality of ongoing human existence, a quality much desired in Christian communal life. And so it has remained through the centuries of Christian history. It is to be emphasized that this was not just a vision of what *Christian* communities should be: it was a vision of what *humanity* could become. We need to ask ourselves now, have we come to that moment in history when this vision of what human existence could be is in fact most needed?

If we are now at the point at which humankind must find some way of growing together into a unified though still thoroughly pluralistic humanity, might this vision provide us with some insight into what we humans must do and become if our more unified peaceful world is ever to come about? At this portentous moment in history, more than ever before, we need visions of the human and understandings of history that will facilitate our movement toward an ordering of life that is at once humane and universal, an ordering in which the integrity and significance of each tradition and each community are acknowledged, and the welfare of every individual is respected. It is important that we lift up into full view every insight and every vision—no matter from what tradition or culture it comes—that might throw light on how to move forward from the ugly inhumanities in which we seem to be trapped toward reconciliation of contending peoples, nations, cultures, religions. New cultural patterns of association and cooperation must be developed, new institutions must be invented, new ideologies that are at once universalistic and truly pluralistic must be created. For these sorts of things to come about, a spirit of self-sacrifice for the well-being of the whole of humanity—and indeed the well-being of the rest of life on planet Earth—will be widely needed, a spirit that can subdue the instincts for self-preservation and self-defense (perhaps among the strongest that we possess) that so dominate our communal and national, as well as our personal, lives.

It is images and stories of communities of reconciliation—in which all recognize that they are "members one of another" (Rom. 12:5) and that they "are all one" (Gal. 3:28), with no discrimination among groups, classes, or sexes—that can focus our attention and our lives on the sorts of commitments we must make and loyalties we must keep if we are to align ourselves with those cosmic and historical forces (whichever ones they may be) that move us creatively (God!) toward a more humane world. Within this context of hopes and dreams, the image of the self-sacrificial Jesus, who gives himself completely so that all may have "abundant life" (John 10:10), stands out in its full pertinence to today's human world. We have here a vivid emblem of the radical transvaluation of our present values that is required if our world of violence and aggressive self-assertion is to become more truly humane and thus more human.[11]

I make no claim that the image/story of Jesus and his early followers is the only one that can inspire the creativity that is needed if we humans are to address effectively the large problems we face today.[12] However, I do want to remind the reader that the history of the many sorts of creativity evoked by this story and image over the last two thousand years is quite remarkable. Some of that history, I admit, has been enormously destructive; creativity can go in many different directions, some of them quite unfortunate, as we have seen. It is with this in mind that I am suggesting that, above all, it is the *radical* themes in the image/story of Jesus, demanding the *transvaluation* of our generally accepted values, that are most likely to inspire new models for the creativity that we humans must now cultivate. Some, of course, continue to invoke the names of Jesus and God to authorize terrible wars and further exploitation of the environment—behaviors clearly opposite to those that can bring peace and reconciliation, love and hope, into our human world. Creativity inspired by the *radical Jesus* should be healing, redemptive, reconciling in our suffering world. The self-giving *agape*-love that Jesus advocated and exemplified during his life will inspire us, we can hope, to find ways that will help create a more truly humane world for the future. The creativity of Jesus continues. . . .

notes

1. Reconceiving the Jesus-Trajectory

1. For discussion of this matter, see Kaufman 1993:chs. 7, 25–26.

2. There are a number of New Testament texts making similar claims; some of these will be discussed later on in this chapter. At the Council of Nicea (325 c.e.) the mythic language of these New Testament texts was given a hard metaphysical interpretation: Jesus Christ was said to be "begotten of the Father uniquely ... of the substance of the Father, God of God, Light of Light, true God of true God, begotten, not made, consubstantial with the Father." (The translation given here is from Hardy 1954:338.) These texts, of course, are all from so-called "orthodox" Christianity. Many Christians, in this early period, held quite different views, as can be seen in some of the Nag Hammadi texts discovered some decades ago and increasingly made available by scholars to a wider public. (See *What Is Gnosticism?* [King 2003a] and *The Gospel of Mary* [King 2003b] for discussion of these matters.)

3. For a sophisticated study of the emergence of christology, its early development, and the importance of that history for contemporary theological work, see Haight 1999:chs. 1–10.

4. This was a central proposal set out in my book *In Face of Mystery: A Constructive Theology* (Kaufman 1993) and later extended and developed in detail in Kaufman 2004. The understanding of theology as *imaginative construction*, which underlies each of these books, is worked out in Kaufman 1995.

5. Christological considerations (important for specifically *Christian* conceptions of God) are left largely undeveloped in Kaufman 2004, though there

are occasional references to Jesus, indicating the openness of this understanding of God to Christian uses. See, e.g., 50f., 60f., 69f., 130n5, 133n12, 139n23.

6. I usually use masculine pronouns when referring to biblical understandings of God, since that usage is found in the Bible, where God is nearly always understood to be male.

7. Cf. Paul: "But now, apart from law, the righteousness of God has been disclosed, and is attested by the law and the prophets, the righteousness of God through faith in Jesus Christ for all who believe. For there is no distinction, since all have sinned and fall short of the glory of God; they are now justified by his grace as a gift, through the redemption that is in Christ Jesus" (Rom. 3:21-24). "For freedom Christ has set us free. Stand firm, therefore, and do not submit again to a yoke of slavery" (Gal. 5:1).

8. Initially the term "Christ" was a title, not a name: it was based on the Greek word *Christos*, which is the Greek translation of *meshiach* ("messiah"), a Hebrew word meaning "anointed by God." This title was occasionally applied to Jesus in Mark's Gospel (written about 70 C.E.) and was used with increasing frequency in the later Gospels. Already when Paul was writing—a generation after Jesus' crucifixion—Jesus was thought of by many Christians as of near divine status (see the discussion below of Jesus-trajectory$_1$), and "Christ" had apparently become virtually a part of Jesus' proper name. So Paul spoke frequently of "Jesus Christ," "Christ Jesus," and often just "Christ." Because of this quite complex meaning of the term "Christ," in order to avoid confusion I stay almost completely with the name Jesus in this book, except when I am discussing a Pauline text where the word "Christ" is employed. But I continue to use the term "christology" when referring to the department of theology that deals with Jesus. For an excellent discussion of the early Christian development and usage of the term "Christ," see Fredricksen 1999:119-54.

9. This is a central contention in Kaufman 2004: see, e.g., 55–58, 71–74, 77–82, 88–92, 102–4.

10. For discussion, see Kaufman 2004:73f.

11. In the next two paragraphs my wording is drawn substantially from Kaufman 2004:69 and 139f.

12. In 1 Cor. 15:4-8 the apostle Paul gives a list (now thought to antecede Paul's conversion by some years) of some of these appearances; and there are many references to Jesus' resurrection throughout the New Testament. For a general review of current historical thinking about Jesus' resurrection, together with a discussion of the significance of the symbol "resurrection" in Christian theology, see Haight 1999:ch. 5. For a somewhat similar review that I put together many years ago, see Kaufman 1968:ch. 28.

13. For discussion of God's "kingship," see Fredricksen 1999:78–89; Haight 1999:61–67, 96–99; Horsley 1987:ch. 7; Sanders 1993:chs. 11–13.

14. Probably written in the early '50s of the first century C.E., about twenty years after Jesus' death.

15. This notion of Jesus-trajectory$_1$ is related in some respects to the concept of "a wider christology," developed in Kaufman 1993:ch. 25. Both of these notions attempt to overcome the sharp distinction between "the historical Jesus" and "the Christ of faith," a distinction frequently made in modern historical and theological writing. The notion of a "wider christology" does this through developing the concept of Christ as "that larger, more complex human reality surrounding and including and following upon the man Jesus" (383); the concept of "Jesus-trajectory$_1$" begins from the other end, so to speak, namely with the ministry of the man Jesus, and proceeds in a more historical manner with the way in which the image of Jesus—in the course of the events following upon his crucifixion—increasingly grows larger and becomes more divine. I entitle this version of the events before and after Jesus' death "Jesus-trajectory$_1$" to distinguish it from "Jesus-trajectory$_2$", which, I will argue, is a more appropriate way to think of these matters today.

16. I omit the birth stories of Jesus here since they *presuppose* Jesus' divine status and were put together, therefore (as most scholars agree), a considerable time after Jesus' death and resurrection, a time when Jesus' divinity was fully acknowledged. Nor is Jesus' "preexistence" taken up at this point; it also presupposes Jesus' divine status and is discussed briefly in n. 27 of ch. 2.

17. For a brief history of the concept of trinity, see Haight 1999:473–80.

18. An excellent detailed discussion of the way in which the titles and other metaphors used by New Testament writers both create and display (in various ways) this historical movement of Jesus into deity is set out in Haight 1999:ch. 6. In chs. 7 through 9 Haight then carries his discussion on into the developments beyond the biblical materials into the classical christologies and soteriologies.

19. "There is salvation in no one else, for there is no other name under heaven given among mortals by which we must be saved" (Acts 4:12).

20. For pertinent quotations from each of these creeds, see p. 2, above (and ch. 1, n. 2); for discussion, see Haight 1999:ch. 10.

21. One well-known New Testament scholar, Marcus Borg, is so carried away by these anthropocentric/anthropomorphic metaphors that he enthusiastically declares that "God is in love with us" (Borg and Wright 1999:142).

22. This argument is elaborated most fully and compactly in Kaufman 2004:esp. ch. 3; see also Kaufman 1993:esp. chs. 21–22.

23. For discussion of this emergence, see ch. 3, below, pp. 64f., 71–75; see also Kaufman 2004:esp. 43–45 and 94–100.

24. It is interesting to note that Paul also was aware that events, especially those connected with God's activity, could occur only when the time was ripe: it was, he says, not until "the fullness of time had come, [that] God sent his Son,

born of a woman, born under the law, in order to redeem those who were under the law" (Gal. 4:4-5).

25. Roger Haight speaks to this point: "The meaning of Jesus is itself not static, but 'overflows,' and keeps on overflowing as Jesus is brought into relationship with ever new situations and problems and peoples. The meaning of Jesus . . . is not, as it were, a given, a substance that takes on new accidental connotations in new relationships. Rather, the new relationships themselves constitute new meanings and relevancies *of Jesus*. Moreover, this does not end in his lifetime. . . . The real historical meaning of Jesus . . . continues to expand through time. Jesus is also related to our time today, and to the multiple situations, peoples, and groups that make up our world" (Haight 1999:56). Robert Neville makes a similar observation: "The first point to make about the historical Jesus is that he is not limited to the individual studied in the quest for the historical Jesus. Rather, the historical Jesus includes the reception of that person by his community after the crucifixion, just as anyone else's identity includes how they are interpreted and responded to. The reception is the historical reality of Jesus, just as the events of Jesus' own subjective life. Furthermore, . . . the real historical Jesus includes all the directions of Christian dispersal around the globe, and in all generations down to now. Jesus is received in the cultural forms of the diverse cultures receiving him. . . . A person's influence and reception is what a historian would include in writing a biography, for instance of Caesar or St. Francis. Jesus' particular self-consciousness is only part of the historical Jesus. . . . So the particular historical reality of Jesus through the ages lies in the complicated dialectic in which the Church in its particular places responds to its imagination of Jesus . . . , based on memories from the gospel of his personal life and as expanded and developed by imagined applications to the new circumstances and places. . . . That Jesus lives from age to age in the imaginations of people in the Church does not make that identity anything less than historical" (Neville 2001:164, 168).

26. For helpful discussions of the current state of the "historical Jesus" question, see Sanders 1993:chs. 1-2, 5-6; Borg and Wright 1998:chs. 1-2; Fredriksen 1999:3-11; Miller 1999:chs. 1-2; Haight 1999:78-87.

27. Although I am inclined toward a more or less pacifist reading of Jesus' actions and teachings, I shall not press that point in this book since it is clearly an anachronistic claim. For some of the pros and cons on this issue, see Horsley 1987:156-63, 261-69, 318-26 ("It would be difficult to claim that Jesus was a pacifist," 326); Fredriksen 1999:241-46; Yoder 1972; Wink 1992. The classical study of the history of Christian pacifism is Bainton 1960; Bainton's contentions about pacifism in the early churches are disputed in Daly 1985. Some specific Jesus-texts bearing on this matter will be discussed in this book, but I am not prepared to judge the complicated historical issues involved in the

question of Jesus' possible pacifism. For more detailed studies on these matters, see the works mentioned in note 26, above.

28. As Baruch Spinoza argued, the concept of evil (like the concept of salvation, which is about being rescued from evil) is basically anthropocentric in character: it refers (in its originary use) to what is destructive of, or threatens to destroy, human existence or well-being, what can make human fulfillment impossible. For discussion of this point, see Kaufman 1993:ch. 24 and Kaufman 1996:87–89.

29. Consider, e.g., Paul: "If anyone proclaims to you a gospel contrary to what you received, let that one be accursed! . . . For I want you to know, brothers and sisters, that the gospel that was proclaimed by me is not of human origin, for I did not receive it from a human source, nor was I taught it, but I received it through a revelation of Jesus Christ" (Gal. 1:9, 11-12).

30. For a New Testament example of such shifting of personal responsibility to a higher authority, consider Paul: "I have been crucified with Christ; and it is no longer I who live, but it is Christ who lives in me" (Gal. 2:19b-20a).

2. Christology: Jesus as Norm

1. See Gal. 1:11-12; 1 Cor. 15:8-10; Acts 9:1-9; 22:6-11; 26:12-18.

2. Ronald Carter argues in *Language and Creativity* (Carter 2004) that human creativity is deeply grounded in our acquisition of *speech*; from early on spoken language was open to creative linguistic developments, and these in turn were—and continue to be—seedbeds for other forms of human creativity. See ch. 3, n. 7.

3. For further discussion of these matters, see Deacon 1997:44–46, 251f., 339–59, 407–10; and Kaufman 2004:44, 84–86, 93–96, 135n9.

4. For discussion of humans as "biohistorical," see ch. 3, below, and also Kaufman 1993:pt. 2.

5. A fuller sketch of these and other aspects of the interconnectedness of human action and freedom, together with their cybernetic extrapolation into values, norms, standards, and criteria for guiding and orienting action, will be found in ch. 3, below; see also Kaufman 1993:chs. 11–15.

6. For further discussion of these matters, see "The Human Niche in Earth's Ecological Order," Kaufman 2006.

7. "For those whom he [God] foreknew he also predestined to be conformed to the image of his Son, in order that he might be the firstborn within a large family" (Rom. 8:29; see 8:28-38).

8. See n. 1. In Paul's own description of this event in Gal. 1, he emphasizes how he was compelled from on high to turn around and give allegiance to Christ.

9. As is well known, the idea of predestination—which presupposes an anthropomorphically conceived God—often eventually developed into hard

doctrines of God's deliberate predestining of every human being either to salvation or to damnation.

10. An excellent study of the development of atonement doctrine and its dehumanizing and demoralizing effects, as well as its inconsistency with the central Christian conviction that God is loving and generous, will be found in Finlan 2005.

11. This point was especially emphasized by the Anabaptists in the Reformation period and by many so-called sectarian groups since, and it seems to be increasingly assumed in many Christian groups today. Some Christians, however (as we have already noted), refuse to accept conclusions of the sort I am drawing here, holding that commitment to Christ cannot be just a matter of human choices and consents, but must be considered as in some sense what God has willed: God predestines some to be believers and others to follow some other path. They are right in claiming that the divine creativity must have its *effects* in and through and with these various choices, but wrong in suggesting that God simply *wills* this or that, and behold it is done. That kind of claim, as we have seen, presupposes some version of an anthropomorphic God ruling from on high, as in the old two-worlds picture. In the theological program with which we are engaged here, these sorts of presuppositions are regarded as no longer intelligible; and arguments based upon them, therefore, do not touch the conceptions with which we are working.

12. See also Kaufman 1993:pt. 2.

13. Roger Haight also emphasizes the necessity to take up today's religious pluralism as a central theme in christological thinking (Haight 1999:152–84, 395–431).

14. The rest of this paragraph and the next one draw heavily from Kaufman 1996:122f. and 118f.

15. For a well-written display of the turns and contradictions in the stories of God in the Old Testament, see *God: A Biography* (Miles 1995). A summary of Miles' conclusions is to be found on pp. 397–408.

16. That "the LORD is a warrior" (Exod. 15:3) is celebrated in the ancient Song of Moses (Exod. 15:1-18).

17. A vivid example is found in 1 Sam. 15. The holy man Samuel (who had anointed Saul as king at Yahweh's command) brings a word from God to Saul: "Go and attack Amalek, and utterly destroy all that they have; . . . kill both man and woman, child and infant, ox and sheep, camel and donkey" (15:3). Despite this order Saul spares Agag, the king of the Amalekites, and the best of the sheep and the cattle (15:8-9). As a result of this disobedience, he is deprived of his kingship (15:26), and then, to make things right again, Samuel "hewed Agag in pieces before the LORD in Gilgal" (15:33). An excellent review and discussion of current scholarly assessments of the biblical texts reporting and celebrating God's extreme violence is found in Collins 2003.

18. For a brief, but somewhat fuller, account of the creation of the biblical conception of God, see Kaufman 2004:3–7.

19. Cf. *Christ: A Crisis in the Life of God* (Miles 2001) for an interesting and insightful "literary" analysis of the dramatic change in *God* as one moves from the Old Testament to the New; see esp. 95–109, 114–30, 175–89, 224f., 252f. (For a brief explanation of Miles' "literary" approach, which treats the Old and New Testaments as presenting biographical accounts of the "life of God," see 247–53.)

20. Most commentators resist strongly this kind of "ontological" reading of the phrase "God is love." (See, e.g., Bultmann 1973:65–74 and Strecker 1996:143–61). They suggest that the phrase cannot properly be reversed into "Love is God" (see, e.g., Strecker 1996:148); and they note that in the Johannine writings there are other similar phrases, such as "God is light" (1 John 1:5) and "God is spirit" (John 4:24), and these similar metaphors are not ordinarily given this kind of weighty meaning. With respect to that point, however, Georg Strecker notes that in 1 John it is "the being that is fundamental to all things and all natures [that] is described with the word *agape*. That which precedes and transcends humanity and its history is love!" (148). Moreover, "the religions that existed in the environment of primitive Christianity did not speak of God in this way" (144). "The statement 'God is love' is something special to Johannine theology" (148). Whatever the writer of 1 John may have originally meant by this phrase, it came to have a life of its own in the course of Christian history, where it has often been regarded as the best way to characterize the God that Christians worship and serve. I am not giving this phrase in 1 John this importance simply because it is scriptural, but rather because it has become so widely employed "as an abbreviated summary of Christian theology" (Strecker:144): it is a phrase that has become a very powerful Christian symbol.

21. Some of these vestiges should probably be judged unfortunate, in light of the dramatic changes we are noting here. For example, Paul (while discussing some Hebrew Bible stories) quotes in Rom. 9:17 a scripture passage in which God declares to Pharaoh, "I have raised you up for the very purpose of showing my power in you" (Exod. 9:16). Paul then states flatly that God "has mercy on whomever he chooses, and he hardens the heart of whomever he chooses"; and he goes on to speak of God's arbitrary power and wrath with no qualms or reservations (Rom. 9:17-24ff.). Jesus also is quoted (in Mark 13) as seemingly taking for granted that, in the coming end time, God will exercise great violent destructive power. And there are many similar images in the visions reported in the Revelation to John, where the wrath, vengefulness, and violence of God are central themes, even though, as many scholars point out (for some references, see Rossing 2005), in Revelation it is "the Lamb" (the nonviolent crucified Jesus) who is to rule the world. Stephen Finlan has shown how these, and many other metaphors in the writings of Paul, developed historically into powerful

atonement doctrines that emphasize the idea of God as violent and seriously distort other central Christian convictions about God (see Finlan 2005:43, 44, 55, 56, 59, 62, 71–79, 98). It is clear that first-century Christianity did not succeed in transforming the inherited image/concept of God as thoroughly as the quoted Johannine texts might suggest; and it is not surprising that literalistic biblical readers of Revelation (and other similar texts) often look forward to Armageddon, when all of the evildoers "left behind" in the "second coming" of Jesus will be punished by God in horribly violent ways. In today's world that religious medicine is much too dangerous to use, though many seem to be gulping it down, especially in the United States.

22. In my recent writings I have refrained nearly always from characterizing creativity in any other way than as *mystery*, thus emphasizing that we simply do not know what creativity is, or why and how it creates. For comparative purposes, however, it would seem that creativity (as I speak of it) must be more like some sort of *activity* than like a person or substance. In this respect speaking of God as creativity is comparable to speaking of God as love.

23. Biologist Ernst Mayr notes that with respect to the appearance of new evolutionary lines of life (new species), specific tendencies and constraints "are the necessary consequence of the unity of the genotype which greatly constrains evolutionary potential" (Mayr 1988:435).

24. In my discussion of Jesus-trajectory$_1$ I sketched the path of conceptual creativity that brought the traditional *image/story* of Jesus into being, but we have not yet considered the creativity that brought Jesus himself into being.

25. "What we ... know past doubting is that John had a crucially important impact on Jesus.... Jesus in some sense received his calling during or just after his baptism" (Fredriksen 1999:191). John the Baptizer and Jesus "both shared the message of the coming Kingdom.... Jesus also baptized, at least for a while" (192). "The reason that the message of John and Jesus sounded in the ears of their contemporaries as prophecy rather than as simply a call to reform was thus not its moral content—... a deeply traditional theme in Jewish piety—but its urgency, the way that they both coupled their call to repentance with their authoritative pronouncement that the times were fulfilled and the Kingdom of heaven was at hand" (195f.). "Jesus shared with John the same urgent message to prepare for God's fast-approaching Kingdom" (197). For an excellent full discussion of these matters, see 184–98.

26. See Kaufman 2004:ch. 3, where these significantly different modalities of creativity that seem to be implied by today's cosmological and evolutionary thinking are described and examined.

27. We should perhaps note here a further feature of this uniqueness of Jesus (as recounted in Jesus-trajectory$_1$), a feature that I have heretofore largely ignored. A few pages back I sketched briefly the kind of pre-history of Jesus that

is appropriate to Jesus-trajectory$_2$. But in Jesus-trajectory$_1$, since Jesus becomes regarded as the divine "second person" of the eternal trinity, a quite different sort of pre-history developed, namely a doctrine of Jesus' "preexistence": God's "Son" had been with the "Father" from all eternity (cf. John 1:1-3; 8:58; Col. 1:15-19; etc.). Given the two-worlds cosmology of Jesus-trajectory$_1$, this is a quite understandable further feature of the conception of Jesus as fully divine. But with our understanding of creativity as a profound evolutionary and historical *mystery*, and of Jesus as in every respect a human being, there is no room for this notion of Jesus' preexistence.

28. See above, ch. 1, end of section II; and Kaufman 2004:69.

29. Heretofore in my theological reflection and writing, I have consistently worked with a trinitarian understanding of God (see, e.g., Kaufman 1968:chs. 6, 17; and Kaufman 1993:ch. 27). I have only recently come to the conclusion that such a view is inevitably anthropocentric and anthropomorphic, and therefore—as a metaphysical claim—must be put into question. However, it is worth noting that the notion of God as *creativity* (as I have been presenting it here) includes within itself the three major themes of the trinitarian doctrine: creativity as ultimate origin of all that is; the distinctive relationship of creativity and Jesus; and the ongoing creativity throughout the whole creation and all of time. In this connection it is interesting to note that the Christian doctrine of the Holy Spirit can be interpreted along lines similar to my proposal of God as ongoing creativity (see Stendahl 1999). So the third person of the trinity is also covered in the notion of God as creativity.

30. This claim is misleading, not only from the perspective of my theological program, but for more traditional theologians as well. Piet Schoonenberg states the pertinent issues clearly: "All our thinking moves from the world to God, and can never move in the opposite direction. Revelation in no way suspends this law. Revelation is the experienced self-communication of God *in* human history, which thereby becomes the history of salvation. With reference to God's Trinity, this law means that the Trinity can never be the point of departure. There is no way that we can draw conclusions from the Trinity to Christ and to the Spirit given to us; only the opposite direction is possible" (quoted in Haight 1999:471). Roger Haight goes on to argue as follows: "We can conclude that trinity is a function of christology. . . . This means that the doctrine of the trinity is not a doctrine that can be isolated, that can, as it were, stand on its own; the doctrine and the theology that generated it are derivative. . . . Trinity is . . . logically derivative from the place that Jesus Christ plays in the Christian life and imagination . . . ; the doctrine of the trinity cannot act as a point of departure for theological reflection; it is not an isolated and autonomous doctrine that can bend back and provide an extrinsic norm for christology; its very content is received from christology" (Haight 1999:479f.).

31. An excellent brief account reminding us that Christianity was never unified but has actually been struggling with internal pluralisms from its very beginning is sketched in Neville 2001:172–85.

32. A quite illuminating typology of some major Jesuses widely influential in Western Christian history is to be found in *Christ and Culture* (Niebuhr 1951). Niebuhr, however, does not work with the distinction between the Jesuses of trajectory$_1$ and trajectory$_2$, which is central for us here. Borg and Wright 1999 discuss issues that bear on some of the similarities and differences of these two trajectories; and there are two informal listings in their book of various kinds of response to Jesus—and thus to the various Jesuses in today's world: in ch. 1 (6f.) and in ch. 4 (7–9). A very interesting account of some highly original *postcolonial* feminist thinking on the question of who is (was?) Jesus is found in Kwok 2005:ch. 7.

33. Kaufman 1993:383. I have used this phrase (and other similar ones) in setting out the "wider christology" that I presented in Kaufman 1993:ch. 25.

3. Humans as Biohistorical Beings

1. For a detailed discussion of the understanding of human beings as fundamentally *biohistorical*, see Kaufman 1993:pt. 2, from which this chapter is largely drawn. See also Kaufman 2004:82–86, 93–100.

2. Geertz 1973:67. The sociobiologists C. J. Lumsden and E. O. Wilson, with their concept of "gene-culture coevolution," appear to concur with this judgment; see Lumsden and Wilson 1983.

3. These five points, and the paragraphs immediately following them, are drawn, with some important modifications, from Kaufman 1993:127–31.

4. Unfortunately, the central symbol of the three Abrahamic religions— God—has been especially susceptible to this sort of destructive use. As we saw in ch. 2, in its beginnings this symbol portrayed God as a "mighty warrior" freeing his devotees from enslavement and protecting them from enemies seeking to destroy them; and throughout history, God has been called upon to continue to exercise his enormous powers in these ways. Although this violent imagery was put into question in the early formative period of the Christian movement, by the time Christianity became the official religion of the Roman Empire, its pacifist tendencies (see ch. 1, n. 27)—though never lost entirely—were largely overwhelmed; and God became a warrior again, protecting his devotees and on occasion even calling for utter destruction of other religious movements (e.g., in the Crusades, the Inquisition, fear of "witches," many fanatical religious groups today). For discussion of this violent side of the symbol "God," see (among a number of related studies) Collins 2003; Juergensmeyer 2000; Nelson-Pallmeyer 2003; Rossing 2005.

5. For discussion, see Kaufman 1993:273–80.

6. George Steiner (2001) argues the importance of retaining the grammatical distinction of genuine *creation* (modeled on the primordial activity of God, and evident in artistic "geniuses" such as Homer, Plato, the architects of Chartres, Shakespeare, Mozart) from the "lower" form of bringing something new into being that is called "inventiveness." "Something within the deep structures of our sensibility balks at the phrasing and concept: 'God invented the universe.' We speak of a major artist as a 'creator', not as an 'inventor' . . . It seems difficult to deny that Thomas Edison 'invented' the light-bulb. . . . And yet a deep-reaching uneasiness or sense of magnification attaches to the statement that Edison 'created' this useful object" (90f.). "We sense 'creation' to be fundamentally above 'invention' . . . the 'creator' exceeds the 'inventor' in the hierarchies of valuation" (92f.). "The Homeric epic, the Platonic dialogue, the Vermeer townscape, the Mozart sonata, do not age and grow obsolescent as do the products of invention" (216). "A lasting work of art, of music, of literature . . . [is] a charged particle, as it were, of the coming into being of being. . . . The great winds of initial creation are at its back" (255f.). I agree that Steiner is making a significant point, but I think that, for an evolutionary understanding of the development of human creativity (a matter that Steiner does not directly address)—and especially in view of Ronald Carter's study of the origins of and continuing occurrence of creativity in the ordinary speaking of humans (Carter 2004; see n. 7, below)—this difference should be regarded as a matter of degree rather than of kind. Indeed, Steiner himself admits that the "formal and existential reach of the two concepts ['creation' and 'invention'] and of their semantic-conceptual fields overlap" (Steiner 2001:103).

7. These developments all occurred in connection with the beginnings of human creativity in and through the emergence of language. Ronald Carter—in his important book *Language and Creativity* (Carter 2004)—contends that "creativity is a pervasive feature of spoken language exchanges . . . and . . . it is a property actively possessed by all speakers and listeners; it is not simply the domain of a few creatively gifted individuals" (6). "Spoken creativity . . . [is] a fundamentally social phenomenon and . . . socioculturally mediated . . . feature of everyday language" (13). "Analysis . . . reveals . . . that creativity is to be located in a wide range of everyday communications, that it is closely linked to humour and wordplay, that it involves affective and interpersonal language choices, and that it occurs more markedly in certain social contexts than others" (12). "It is the essentially unconscious, often unplanned, nature of speech, the fact that the system is so mobile and in a constant state of flux, . . . responsible to the smallest and most subtle changes in contextual environment, that makes it so fascinating. . . . Spoken language thus represents *language at full stretch*, so much so that even the most detailed, faithful and sympathetic transcription cannot hope to capture it" (57). "Creative language may be a default condition, a norm of use

from which ordinary, routine 'non-creative' exchanges constitute an abnormal departure" (214).

8. This paragraph is drawn largely from Kaufman 1993:167f.

9. For a more detailed discussion of these matters, see Kaufman 1993:143–62. In some cultures this sense of *personal* responsibility seems to be almost totally absent. See Mühlhäusler and Harré 1990:ch. 7.

10. For further discussion of "I" and "we," see Kaufman 1993:149–57, 165–67, 212–15.

11. Jared Diamond has described well, in his recent book *Collapse* (Diamond 2005), the tragic total breakdown, on Easter Island, of an obviously very complex human life and culture. In this book he also examines carefully a number of other striking examples of human sociocultural breakdown.

12. Niebuhr 1963 has called attention to this double meaning of "responsibility" (see esp. ch. 1 where he lays out an original and illuminating ethics of responsibility to which I am deeply indebted).

13. The rest of this paragraph draws heavily on Kaufman 1993:147; also see the diagram on p. 145.

14. See Kaufman 1993:chs. 11–13.

15. For a full discussion of these distinctions, see Kaufman 1993:183–91; much of this present paragraph and the preceding one has been drawn from pp. 185–87.

16. Ludwig Wittgenstein has worked out in detail this notion of a "world-picture" that is presupposed and taken for granted in all of our experiencing, thinking, imagining, daydreaming, and acting. See Wittgenstein 1969.

17. These books are both based on and extensions of my larger attempt to present a revisionary conception of Christian theology and faith for today, in Kaufman 1993.

18. This discussion of freedom draws heavily on Kaufman 1993:170–75.

4. Creativity Is *Good News!*

1. Through the mouth of Isaiah, it was believed, God had long ago announced that he was going to do "new things" from time to time: "I am about to do a new thing; now it springs forth, do you not perceive it? ... From this time forward I make you hear new things, hidden things that you have not known. They are created now, not long ago; before today you have never heard of them" (43:19a; 48:6b-7a). And Jeremiah had prophesied that God would eventually make a new covenant with Israel (Jer. 31:31-34). In this connection it is interesting to note that a central point in Paul's preaching was that "if anyone is in Christ, there is a *new creation*; everything old has passed away; see, everything has become new! All this is from God" (2 Cor. 5:17-18a; emphasis

added). The idea of God's ongoing creativity—God's bringing into being the *new*—is very much alive in the Bible.

2. For example, consider the growing interest in the fresh ideas and practices concerning *peacebuilding* and *restorative justice* proposed by some Mennonites and others with pacifist backgrounds; see John Paul Lederach 1997 and 2005, and Howard Zehr 1990. Consider also the work of Walter Wink 1992 and the far-ranging radicality of postcolonial feminist theological ideas and activities, as recounted in Kwok Pui Lan 2005.

3. See ch. 3, above, n. 2.

4. See Kaufman 2004:ch. 3.

5. Ibid., 43–45, 94–100.

6. Cf. Ps. 90:4:"For a thousand years in your sight are like yesterday when it is past, or like a watch in the night."

7. Quoted above in ch. 2, section II.

8. See ch. 3, above, sections I and II.

9. For some discussion of this, see Kaufman 1993:156–58.

10. Much of the wording of this paragraph is drawn from Kaufman 1996:116f.

11. This paragraph draws heavily on Kaufman 1993:407, and in part on p. 403.

12. With the ending of Western colonialism, a great deal of fresh thinking about the basic ordering and orienting of human life around the globe has been going on—in previously colonized sectors of the world and also in America and Europe. Some of this"postcolonial" activity and thinking (especially among feminist theologians) is inspired by the basic Christian stories and the profound guilt about the evils of Western imperialism felt today by many Europeans and Americans. But—not surprisingly—much is also grounded in non-Christian religious and cultural traditions as well, and is, quite justifiably, deeply critical of many traditional Christian attitudes, ideas, and behaviors. An excellent, well-organized review of much of this material and its significance for theology is found in Kwok 2005.

bibliography bibliography

Ashbrook, James B., and Carol Rausch Albright. 1997. *The Humanizing Brain: Where Religion and Neuroscience Meet*. Cleveland: Pilgrim.

Bainton, Roland. 1960. *Christian Attitudes toward War and Peace: A Historical Survey and Critical Re-evaluation*. New York: Abingdon.

Borg, Marcus, and N. T. Wright. 1999. *The Meaning of Jesus: Two Visions*. San Francisco: Harper.

Bultmann, Rudolf. 1958. *Jesus Christ and Mythology*. New York: Scribner.

———. 1973. *The Johannine Epistles*. Philadelphia: Fortress Press.

Carter, Ronald. 2004. *Language and Creativity: The Art of Common Talk*. London: Routledge.

Collins, John J. 2003. "The Zeal of Phinehas: The Bible and the Legitimation of Violence," *Journal of Biblical Literature* 122:3–21.

Daly, Robert J., ed. 1985. *Christians and the Military: The Early Experience*. By John Helgeland, Robert J. Daly, and J. Patout Burns. Philadelphia: Fortress Press.

Deacon, Terrence. 1997. *The Symbolic Species: The Co-evolution of Language and the Brain*. New York: Norton.

Diamond, Jared 2005. *Collapse: How Societies Choose to Fail or Succeed*. New York: Viking.

Ehrenreich, Barbara. 1997. *Blood Rites: Origins and History of the Passions of War*. New York: Henry Holt.

Finlan, Stephen. 2005. *Problems with Atonement: The Origin and Controversy about the Atonement Doctrine*. Collegeville, Minn.: Liturgical.

Fredriksen, Paula. 1999. *Jesus of Nazareth, King of the Jews*. New York: Knopf.

———. 2000. *From Jesus to Christ: The Origins of the New Testament Images of Christ*. 2nd Ed. New Haven: Yale University Press.

Geertz, Clifford. 1973. *The Interpretation of Cultures*. New York: Basic.

Haight, Roger. 1999. *Jesus: Symbol of God*. Maryknoll, N.Y.: Orbis.

Hardy, Edward R. ed. 1954. *Christology of the Later Fathers*. Library of Christian Classics, vol. 3. Philadelphia: Westminster.

Horsley, Richard. 1987. *Jesus and the Spiral of Violence*. San Francisco: Harper & Row.

Juergensmeyer, Mark. 2000. *Terror in the Mind of God: The Global Rise of Religious Violence*. Berkeley: University of California Press.

Kaufman, Gordon D. 1968. *Systematic Theology: A Historicist Perspective*. New York: Scribner.

———. 1972. *God the Problem*. Cambridge: Harvard University Press.

———. 1993. *In Face of Mystery: A Constructive Theology*. Cambridge: Harvard University Press.

———. 1995. *An Essay on Theological Method*. 3rd ed. New York: Oxford University Press. (1st ed. 1975. Scholars Press.)

———. 1996. *God—Mystery—Diversity: Christian Theology in a Pluralistic World*. Minneapolis: Fortress Press.

———. 2004. *In the beginning . . . Creativity*. Minneapolis: Fortress Press.

———. 2006. The Human Niche in Earth's Ecological Order. In *Theology That Matters: Ecology, Economy, and God*, ed. Darby Kathleen Ray, 108–20. Minneapolis: Fortress Press.

King, Karen. 2003a. *What Is Gnosticism?* Cambridge: Harvard University Press.

———. 2003b. *The Gospel of Mary of Magdala*. Santa Rosa, Calif.: Polebridge.

Kwok Pui Lan. 2005. *Postcolonial Imagination and Feminist Theology*. Louisville: Westminster John Knox.

Lederach, John Paul. 1997. *Building Peace: Sustainable Reconciliation in Divided Societies*. Washington, D.C.: United States Institute of Peace Press.

———. 2005. *The Moral Imagination: The Art and Soul of Building Peace*. New York: Oxford University Press.

Lumsden, C. J., and E. O. Wilson. 1983. *Promethean Fire: Reflections on the Origin of Mind*. Cambridge: Harvard University Press.

Mayr, Ernst. 1988. *Toward a New Philosophy of Biology*. Cambridge: Harvard University Press.

Miles, Jack. 1995. *God: A Biography*. New York: Knopf.

———. 2001. *Christ: A Crisis in the Life of God*. New York: Knopf.

Miller, Robert. 1999. *The Jesus Seminar and Its Critics*. Santa Rosa, Calif.: Polebridge.

Mühlhäusler, Peter, and Rom Harré. 1990. *Pronouns and People: The Linguistic*

Construction of Social and Personal Identity. Oxford: Blackwell.

Nelson-Pallmeyer, Jack. 2003. *Is Religion Killing Us? Violence in the Bible and the Quran.* Harrisburg, Pa.: Trinity Press International.

Neville, Robert C. 2001. *Symbols of Jesus: A Christology of Symbolic Engagement.* Cambridge: Cambridge University Press.

Niebuhr, H. Richard. 1951. *Christ and Culture.* New York: Harper.

———. 1960. *Radical Monotheism and Western Culture.* New York: Harper.

———. 1963. *The Responsible Self.* New York: Harper & Row.

Rossing, Barbara R. 2005. "Apocalyptic Violence and Politics: End-Times Fiction for Jews and Christians," *Reflections* 92, no. 1:16–22.

Sanders, E. P. 1993. *The Historical Figure of Jesus.* London: Penguin.

Spinoza, Baruch. [1677] 1989. *Ethics.* Translated by Andrew Boyle. Revised by H. R. Parkinson. London: Dent.

Steiner, George. 2001. *Grammars of Creation.* London: Faber & Faber.

Stendahl, Krister. 1999. *Energy for Life: Reflections on a Theme; Come, Holy Spirit— Renew the Whole Creation.* Brewster, Mass.: Paraclete.

Strecker, Georg. 1995. *The Johannine Letters.* Minneapolis: Fortress Press.

White, Andrew Dickson [1886] 1993. *A History of the Warfare of Science with Theology in Christendom.* Buffalo, N.Y.: Prometheus.

Wieman, Henry Nelson. 1946. *The Source of Human Good.* Chicago: University of Chicago Press.

Wink, Walter. 1992. *Engaging the Powers.* Minneapolis: Fortress Press.

Wittgenstein, Ludwig. 1969. *On Certainty.* New York: Harper & Row.

Wright, G. Ernest. 1952. *God Who Acts.* London: SCM.

Yoder, John Howard. 1972. *The Politics of Jesus.* Grand Rapids, Mich.: Eerdmans.

Zehr, Howard. 1990. *Changing Lenses: A New Focus for Crime and Justice.* Scottdale, Pa.: Herald.

index of subjects and names

index   index of scripture

141